YOU'RE HIRED! LEVERAGING YOUR NETWORK

JOB SEARCH STRATEGIES THAT WORK

RAE A. STONEHOUSE

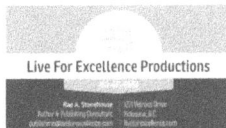

Live For Excellence Productions

Rae A. Stonehouse
Author & Publishing Consultant
publisher@raestonehouse.com

Westwood Circle
Kelowna, BC
RaeStonehouse.com

1. COPYRIGHT

2. CONNECT WITH US

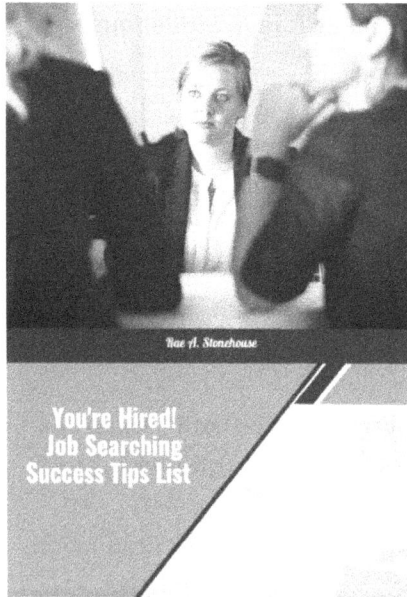

Subscribe to our **You're Hired! Job Search Strategies That Work Newsletter** to receive job searching sage advice from Rae A. Stonehouse and receive **You're Hired! Job Searching Success Tips List**, a free e-book providing you with 55 tips to landing your next job.

http://eepurl.com/ghp73f

Visit us on the web at http://yourehirednow.com.

Check out our **Jobs Now Blog** @ http//yourehirednow.com for job searching advice to frequently asked questions.

For even more job searching tips & techniques, join us on **Facebook** https://www.facebook.com/jobstrategiesthatwork/

Twitter: https://twitter.com/yourehirednow

∾

WELCOME!

Hi there! Welcome to **You're Hired! Leveraging Your Network - Job Search Strategies That Work.**

Make no mistake. Searching for work… is work!

It takes time, effort and a lot of self-motivation to succeed in your search.

While you have your skills and experience in place to apply for and land your dream job, or one that leads you to it, searching for a job requires a whole different set of skills.

In many job markets being invited for an interview can be like winning a lottery. Your resume likely got you in the door, now you need to wow the Interviewer and do your best in the interview to land the job.

This book focuses on strategies for *building and leveraging your network* to maximize your job searching effectiveness and is excerpted and expanded upon, from my book **You're Hired! Job Search Strategies That Work.**

Nobody can make a promise if you follow their program, you will be guaranteed the results you are looking for and I won't either.

However, I'm confident if you follow the strategies outlined in this book, your chances of being successful in landing a job are increased.

From my experience, one of the biggest problems job seekers often face is they feel they are coming from an inferior position and they don't have a lot of personal power. The belief being the Employer has the superior position and has all the power.

Yes, they have the job and they have the power to give you the job... or not.

What you may not realize is many Hiring Managers are under similar pressures as you, the job seeker. They have the pressure of finding the right candidate for the vacancy they need to fill.

They are accountable to their superiors should the person they hire not work out. It has been said an inappropriate hire can cost the organization an additional 30 to 50 percent over the job position's annual wage. This would include lost productivity incurred when the new hire is oriented, the cost of advertising for new applicants and the time taken to interview and follow up with applicants.

Hiring managers are under pressure to hire the right candidate.

Your task is to become the *only* choice. The *right* choice!

As I mentioned earlier, we are likely not experts at searching for jobs and landing one. It isn't something we do on a regular basis.

As I researched the content for my book **You're Hired! Job Search Strategies That Work**, I found the problem is compounded by a lack of hard facts on what are the best-practices for job searching.

I'm reminded of an old parable about a group of blind men were required to touch an elephant and to describe their observations.

Each one felt a different part, but only one part, such as a tusk or the trunk. When they compared notes, they learned they were in complete disagreement.

I found the same to be true when researching strategic job searching skills.

Each webpage from my search results on the internet spoke from the perspective of the writer whether they were a resume writer, an Employer Hiring Manager, recruiter, etc.

Much the same as the blind men describing what an elephant looks like, their advice is from their perspective. That makes sense to me. We all create our own reality. My reality is completely different from anyone else's.

The problem is the job search 'experts' state their observations as hard facts. They believe what they write is true. And then the next article you read, will dispute what the first expert had said and they will present their truths.

How can something be both true and false at the same time? You must never do this. You must always do this.

Same advice. Can something be both yes and no?

I don't consider myself an expert at job searching.

What I am very good at though is taking subjects people struggle with, finding better, easier ways to do things and breaking it down to basic strategies that work.

I create *systems* to solve *problems*.

Years ago, I moved my family across Canada to a city where I didn't know anyone.

I had a brand-new home built for me, but I didn't have a job waiting for me when I got there.

At the time, the new location was very hostile towards people who had moved from the east to the west coast.

I often heard "you Easterners come out here and steal our jobs…"

I found jobs were limited. I found getting an interview for a position I had applied for was like winning a lottery.

I also found my new geographical area had what they called a 'Sunshine Tax.'

As a desirable place to live, the cost of living is higher and employers believe they can get away with paying their employees lower wages. The idea being you the worker should be grateful to have a job and the employer can get away with paying you less.

"If you don't want the job, somebody else will!"

I got so tired of hearing about stealing local jobs I started to change my story when I attended local business networking events.

Instead of saying I was *unemployed*, I would say I had *retired* early.

I was 39 years old and the illusion I had retired early seem to resolve the 'you Easterners' complaint.

However, I used to add "if the right job came along, I would likely consider going back to work."

It was offered somewhat tongue in cheek.

It took me a good six months to land a job. It wasn't as good a job as I had hoped.

It was a compromise until something better came along.

I describe my employment experience at my new location as being like a roller coaster ride.

I went from being unemployed, to employed. I went from not getting enough hours to getting too many.

I went from being employed to being laid off.

I went from being employed to being self-employed.

Self-employment ended when I came back from a vacation to find my only client had sold their business i.e. a vocational school and the new owners had no idea who I was or had need of my services.

Back to being unemployed.

Then I got a job in another city. It was a 90-mile round trip, daily.

I went from being at the employer's beck and call for three years working as many hours as I could as a casual staff. Then I got fired!

Then I got *unfired* and a new job, same company, a few blocks away.

I went from full time to no time to part time to even more part time. Then less time and even less time.

I had to tell my manager I couldn't afford to stay and I couldn't afford to go.

We solved the problem by me picking up hours from another worker who wanted to work less.

The downside is I work a lot of night shifts and it is still a 90 mile, 150-kilometre round trip for work.

I think you can see why I call it a roller coaster ride.

Over the years, I have been invited to numerous job search training programs as a guest speaker, promoting the value of public speaking skills to the job search and interviewing process as well as networking skills.

Throughout this book, I will be providing you with what I consider being the best practices for leveraging and building your network.

Some content may disagree with what the so-called experts would say but then again... the next one would likely agree with me.

If you are a sports fan, you will recognize that any sport has a set of rules and varying degrees of competition.

Searching for a job, your job, is a competitive situation.

It could come down to two or more possible candidates, hopefully you, being one of them, having very similar credentials and qualifications.

If there was ever a time self-promotional skills and self-confidence would come into play, it would be in the job searching and interviewing process.

Being able to effectively promote yourself can make the difference between landing the job and a 'thank you very much, but we won't be hiring you at this time."

Welcome aboard and I hope you enjoy our journey together!

SECTION ONE: CREATING & LEVERAGING YOUR NETWORK WEB

3. INTRODUCTION TO YOUR NETWORK WEB

W elcome to Section One. In this lesson, we look at how to create and use your *Network Web* to help search for your job.

We are also going to look at some strategies to help you when you are out there networking. I call them power networking strategies.

But before we do so, it is probably a good idea to explain what a Network Web is and why you should create one.

In the not too distant past there was a principle identified as *Six Degrees of Separation*.

According to Wikipedia... Six degrees of separation is the idea all living things and everything else in the world are six or fewer steps away from each other so a chain of "a friend of a friend" statements can be made to connect any two people in a maximum of six steps.

It was originally set out by Frigyes Karinthy in 1929. Karinthy was apparently a Hungarian Author.

With the rapid development of on-line social media venues, it has been said the degrees of separation that connect you to almost anybody in the world is now down to three degrees.

If you are on Linkedin, and you should be, you can easily see as your number of 1st degree connections increase, your 2nd and 3rd degree connections increase exponentially. Your 3rd degree connections could easily be in the millions.

So how do we take advantage of this worldwide interconnectedness?

The answer to that question while it is an easy one, does take some work.

The *Network Web* is a tool that helps you draw upon your personal network to find the ideal job you are looking for. Your ideal job may not be posted yet, in fact, it may not even be created yet. Your Network Web can help put you in front of decision makers and key people that are in the position to hire you.

Step One is to make a list of your personal categories.

These are your interests and the organizations, formal and informal that you belong to.

These may include hobbies, family, church, professional organizations, sports teams, current and past employment.

Create a page for each of the above categories as well as any others you can think of.

Once you have completed the task, please go to the next step in this strategy.

Step Two is to make a list of people you know in each category, start with a list of 10 names for each organization or interest category and then add 10 more if possible.

Don't worry about considering if you have seen them recently or not.

At this point, your task is to generate as many names as you can.

When you have completed this task please go to the next step in this strategy.

Step Three: For illustrative purposes, we will use this drawing. It is basically a web with you at the centre and four circles located on the web.

You should create a document with the names of the circles as your headings.

First Circle: The *Crisis Circle* is closest to the centre of the Web.

These are the people you can really count on.

You should have at least four people who will be supportive in the event of death, illness, divorce or bankruptcy. They can include family, friends, your doctor or lawyer.

The Second Circle: This is your *buddy circle.*

Friends you have fun with, the people who accept you for who you are. There should be at least three people in this circle.

The Third Circle: This is your *professional circle.*

People who you know professionally, can provide reference letters and can speak about the quality of your work and character. You need at least 12 people in this category.

The Fourth Circle: This is your *casual friends* circle.

People you can share ideas with. You may work with them or know them through organizations or volunteer work. Some may become closer friends and eventually form part of the more inner and intimate circles.

NOW YOU HAVE SOME WORK TO DO.

Create a list of people under the four circle's headings e.g. My Crisis Circle... My Buddies Circle ...

Up to this point we haven't factored in our Linkedin connections.

Likely, many of your Linkedin connections will fit into your Third Circle, your *professional circle*.

Once you have gone though your Linkedin connections, go through your other social media accounts and your e-mail address book and write down names.

You'll be surprised at how quickly the list grows.

IN THE NEXT CHAPTER, WE LEARN HOW TO LEVERAGE THE CONNECTIONS you have just identified.

≈

"ONE OF THE BEST PLACES TO START TO TURN YOUR LIFE AROUND IS BY **doing whatever appears on your mental 'I should' list." Jim Rohn**

"ALWAYS DO MORE THAN IS REQUIRED OF YOU." — GEORGE S. PATTON

"IF YOU BELIEVE IN WHAT YOU ARE DOING, THEN LET NOTHING HOLD YOU **up in your work. Much of the best work of the world has been done against seeming impossibilities. The thing is to get the work done." — Dale Carnegie**

"DESIRE IS THE KEY TO MOTIVATION, BUT IT'S THE DETERMINATION AND **commitment to an unrelenting pursuit of your goal - a commitment to excellence - that will enable you to attain the success you seek." — Mario Andretti**

4. LEVERAGING YOUR CONNECTIONS

I n this chapter, we delve deeper into networking and how we can *leverage* our connections as a powerful job searching strategy.

YOU MAY THINK YOU DON'T KNOW ANYONE WHO CAN HELP YOU WITH your job search. But you know more people than you think, and there's a very good chance at least a few of these people know someone who can give you career advice or point you to a job opening.

You'll never know if you don't ask!

Some Job Search Coaches will tell you leveraging your network is the most effective strategy you can use to find your ideal job.

The **Network Web** is a powerful tool. You'll be amazed at all the contacts you do have, and can identify the gaps in the network.

With your goal of finding suitable employment in mind you can ask:

- Who do I need to know?
- Who do I need to bring into my circle?
- And who do I know who can introduce them to me?

Reach out to your network

All the connections in the world won't help you find a job if no one knows about your situation.

Once you've drawn up your list, start making contact with the people in your network. Let them know that you're looking for a job.

Be specific about what kind of work you're looking for and ask them if they have any information or know anyone in a relevant field.

Don't assume certain people won't be able to help. You may be surprised by who they know.

FIGURE OUT WHAT YOU *WANT* BEFORE YOU START NETWORKING

Networking is most effective when you have specific employer targets and career goals. It's hard to get leads with a generic "Let me know if you hear of anything" request.

You may think you'll have better job luck if you leave yourself open to all the possibilities, but the reality is this 'openness' creates a black hole that sucks all the networking potential out of the connection.

A *generic* networking request for a job is worse than no request at all because you can lose a networking contact and opportunity.

Asking for *specific* information, leads, or an interview is much more focused and easier for the networking source.

If you're having trouble focusing your job search, you can turn to close friends and family members for help, but avoid contacting more distant people in your network until you've set clear goals.

Start with your references

When you are looking for a job, start with your references.

Your best references—the people who like you and can endorse your abilities, track record, and character—are *major networking hubs.* Contact each one of your references to network about your possibilities and affirm their agreement to be your reference.

We discuss strategies for working with your references in greater detail in Section Four but here are a few quick points.

- Describe your goals and seek their assistance.
- Keep them informed on your job search progress.
- Prepare them for any calls from potential employers.
- Let them know what happened and thank them for their help regardless of the outcome.

If you're nervous about making contact—either because you're uncomfortable asking for favours or embarrassed about your employment situation—try to keep the following things in mind:

It feels good to help others. Most people will gladly assist you if they can. People like to give advice and be recognized for their expertise.

Almost everyone knows what it's like to be out of work or looking for a job. They'll sympathize with your situation.

Unemployment can be isolating and stressful. By connecting with others, you're sure to get some much-needed encouragement, fellowship, and moral support. Reconnecting with the people in your network can be fun—even if you have an agenda.

The more this feels like a chore the more tedious and anxiety-ridden the process will be.

Focus on building relationships

Networking is a give-and-take process that involves making connections, sharing information, and asking questions. It's a way of relating to others, not a *technique* for getting a job or a favour.

You don't have to hand out your business cards on street corners, cold call everyone on your contact list, or work a room of strangers. All you have to do is reach out.

Be authentic. In any job search or networking situation, being you—the real you—should be your goal. Hiding who you are or suppressing your true interests and goals will only hurt you in the long run.

Pursuing what you want and not what you think others will like, will always be more fulfilling and ultimately more successful.

Be considerate. If you're reconnecting with an old friend or colleague, take the time to get through the catching-up phase before you blurt out your need. On the other hand, if this person is a busy professional you don't know well, be respectful of his or her time and come straight out with your request.

Ask for *advice*, not a job. Don't ask for a job, a request comes with a lot of pressure.

You want your contacts to become allies in your job search, not make them feel ambushed, so ask for information or insight instead. If they're able to hire you or refer you to someone who can, they will.

If not, you haven't put them in the uncomfortable position of turning you down or telling you they can't help. Be specific in your request.

Before you go off and reconnect with everyone you've ever known, get your act together and do a little homework. Be prepared to articulate *what* you're looking for:

- Is it a reference?
- An insider's take on the industry?
- A referral?
- An introduction to someone in the field?

Also make sure to provide an update on your qualifications and recent professional experience.

SLOW DOWN AND ENJOY THE JOB NETWORKING PROCESS

The best race car drivers are masters of slowing down.

They know the fastest way around the track is by slowing down going into the turns, so they can accelerate sooner as they're heading into the straightaway.

As you're networking, keep this "Slow in, fast out" racing mantra in mind. Effective networking is not something that should be rushed.

This doesn't mean you shouldn't try to be efficient and focused, but hurried, *emergency* networking is not conducive to building relationships for mutual support and benefit.

When you network, you should slow down, be present, and try to enjoy the process. This will speed up your chances for success in the job-hunting race.

Just because you have an agenda doesn't mean you can't enjoy reconnecting.

DON'T BE A HIT-AND-RUN NETWORKER

Don't be a hit-and-run networker: connecting, getting what you want, and then disappearing, never to be heard from until the next time you need something.

Invest in your network by following up and providing feedback to those who were kind enough to offer their help. Thank them for their referral and assistance. Let them know whether you got the interview or the job. Or use the opportunity to report on the lack of success or the need for additional help.

Evaluate the quality of your network

IF YOUR NETWORKING EFFORTS DON'T SEEM TO BE GOING ANYWHERE, you may need to evaluate the quality of your network. Take some time to think about your network's strengths, weaknesses and opportunities.

Without such an evaluation, there is little chance your network will adapt to your needs and your future goals. You may not notice how bound you are to history, or how certain connections are holding you back. And you may miss opportunities to branch out and forge new ties that will help you move forward.

Taking inventory of your network and where it is lacking is time well spent. If you feel your network is out of date, then it's time to upgrade! Your mere awareness of your needs will help you connect you with new and more relevant contacts and networks.

TAKE ADVANTAGE OF BOTH 'STRONG' AND 'WEAK' TIES

Everyone has both 'strong' and 'weak' ties.

Strong ties occupy that inner circle and weak ties are less established. Adding people to networks is time consuming, especially strong ties. It requires an investment of time and energy to have multiple 'best friends.' Trying to stay in touch with new acquaintances is just as challenging. But adding new 'weak tie' members gives your network vitality and even more cognitive flexibility—the ability to consider new ideas and options.

New relationships invigorate the network by providing a connection to new networks, viewpoints, and opportunities.

~

IN THE NEXT CHAPTER, WE EXPLORE TIPS FOR STRENGTHENING YOUR JOB search network.

"IF YOU ARE NOT TOO LARGE FOR THE PLACE YOU OCCUPY, YOU ARE TOO small for it." — James A. Garfield

"MAKE A STRONG AND PERMANENT COMMITMENT TO INVEST YOUR talents only in pursuits that deserve your best efforts." -- Nido Qubein

"DON'T SAY, 'IF I COULD, I WOULD.' SAY, 'F I CAN, I WILL.'" — Jim Rohn

5. TIPS FOR STRENGTHENING YOUR JOB SEARCH NETWORK

T ap into your strong ties. Your strong ties will logically and trustingly lead to new weak ties that build a stronger network.

Use your existing network to add members and reconnect with people. Start by engaging the people in your trusted inner circle to help you fill in the gaps in your network.

Think about where you want to go. Your network should reflect where you're going, not just where you've been. Adding people to your network who reflect issues, jobs, industries, and areas of interest is essential.

If you are a new graduate or a career changer, join the professional associations that represent your desired career path. Attending conferences, reading journals, and keeping up with the lingo of your desired field can prepare you for where you want to go.

Make the process of connecting a priority. Make connecting a habit—part of your lifestyle. Connecting is just as important as your exercise routine. It breathes life into you and gives you confidence.

Find out how your network is doing in this environment, what steps they are taking, and how you can help. As you connect, the world will feel smaller and a small world is much easier to manage.

Take the time to maintain your network

Maintaining your job-search network is just as important as building it.

Accumulating new contacts can be beneficial, but only if you have the time to nurture the relationships. Avoid the irrational impulse to meet as many new people as possible.

The key is quality rather than quantity. Focus on cultivating and maintaining your existing network. You're sure to discover an incredible array of information, knowledge, expertise, and opportunities.

Schedule time with your key contacts

List the people who are crucial to your network—people you know who can and have been very important to you. Invariably, there will be some you have lost touch with.

Reconnect and then schedule a regular meeting or phone call. You don't need a reason to get in touch. It will always make you feel good and provide you with an insight or two.

PRIORITIZE THE REST OF YOUR CONTACTS

Keep a running list of people you need to reconnect with. People whose view of the world you value. People you'd like to get to know better or whose company you enjoy.

Prioritize these contacts and then schedule time into your regular routine so you can make your way down the list.

TAKE NOTES ON THE PEOPLE IN YOUR NETWORK

Collecting cards and filing them is a start. But maintaining your contacts, new and old, requires updates. Add notes about their families, their jobs, their interests, and their needs.

Unless you have a photographic memory, you won't remember all of this information unless you write it down. Put these updates and notes on the back of their business cards or input them into your contact database.

FIND WAYS TO RECIPROCATE

Always remember successful networking is a *two-way* street. Your ultimate goal is to cultivate mutually beneficial relationships.

That means giving as well as receiving.

Send a thank-you note, ask them about their family, email an article you think they might be interested in, and check in periodically to see how they're doing. By nurturing the relationship through your job search and beyond, you'll establish a strong network of people you can count on for ideas, advice, feedback, and support.

~

IN THE NEXT FEW CHAPTERS WE LOOK CLOSER AT SOME STRATEGIES TO maximize our effectiveness when out there networking... person to person.

~

"BELIEVE AND ACT AS IF IT WERE IMPOSSIBLE TO FAIL."— CHARLES F. Kettering

"MAKE SURE THE OUTSIDE OF YOU IS A GOOD REFLECTION OF THE INSIDE of you." Jim Rohn

"IT TAKES LESS TIME TO DO THINGS RIGHT THAT TO EXPLAIN WHY YOU did it wrong." — Henry Wadsworth Longfellow

"YOU HAVE THE ABILITY, RIGHT NOW, TO EXCEED ALL YOUR PREVIOUS levels of accomplishment." — Brian Tracy

"TO ATTRACT ATTRACTIVE PEOPLE, YOU MUST BE ATTRACTIVE. TO attract powerful people, you must be powerful. To attract committed people, you must be committed. Instead of going to work on them, you go to work on yourself. If you become, you can attract." — Jim Rohn

6. DRESS FOR SUCCESS

M ost of us have likely been told from a very early age "You shouldn't judge a book by its cover."

Yet we do it every day, often in the first few seconds of having met someone.

We automatically determine whether they are a danger to us, whether we would want to have a conversation with them, whether we would want them as a mate... or to mate with.

We do it automatically.

It's part of being human and our judgement is often made with the clothing the person is wearing as one of our decision-making criteria. Being dressed inappropriately for a given situation can set you apart so people do not want to approach you to converse.

If you are shy, having somebody come up to you to talk can be a lot easier than having to make the approach yourself. So, don't reduce your chances by dressing wrong.

Wrong? What does that mean?

There is a lot of room for interpretation. What is wrong for one person is right for another. Many people like to express themselves through colourful clothing or cutting-edge fashion.

Many people don't have a clue when it comes to dressing for the occasion.

I once attended a black- tie gala awards event. I was in a tuxedo as was my colleague. We observed some men in their cleanest blue jeans with a black string tie.

I think they missed the point.

My suggestion would be if you were attending a business networking event, then 'business casual' would be appropriate. This can become even more casual in hot climates.

If everyone is wearing shorts and you are in your tuxedo, you may get attention but perhaps not the kind you wanted.

As for dressing for success, it has been proven over and over most people feel better about themselves when they're dressed up. You need every advantage you can get when you are out there networking, marketing yourself.

Don't shut the door in your face before it is even opened. People do judge others by their clothing, don't let them judge you without talking to you first.

❧

IN OUR NEXT CHAPTER, WE LOOK AT BUSINESS CARD PRESENTATION AND etiquette.

❧

"DRESS FOR SUCCESS. IMAGE IS VERY IMPORTANT. PEOPLE JUDGE YOU BY the way you look on the outside." — Brian Tracy

"IF YOU BELIEVE YOU CAN, AND BELIEVE IT STRONGLY ENOUGH, YOU'LL BE surprised at what you can do." — Nido Qubein

"YOUR ATTITUDE IS AN EXPRESSION OF YOUR VALUES, BELIEFS AND expectation." — Brian Tracy

"IF YOU BELIEVE IN WHAT YOU ARE DOING, THEN LET NOTHING HOLD YOU up in your work. Much of the best work of the world has been done against seeming impossibilities. The thing is to get the work done." — Dale Carnegie

7. BUSINESS CARD PRESENTATION & ETIQUETTE

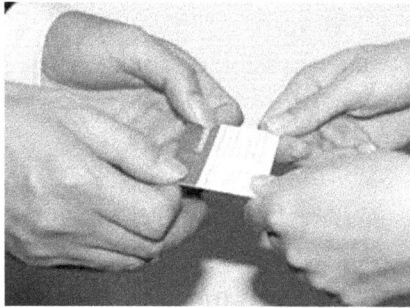

I n an earlier chapter in this section, we made mention a couple times about using business cards in your networking activities.

Now we are going to take a closer look at business card presentation and etiquette. If you are planning on doing some serious networking, you should have business cards available to present to another.

Not having a card to present may be a missed opportunity for you.

Besides serving as an introduction for you, they will serve as a visual prompt to remind the other person they met and spoke to you.

It can be difficult to think of using business cards when you are searching for work and you aren't in business. It might help to think of them as being 'calling' cards.

Their purpose is to provide your name and contact information for anyone who might want to get in contact with you.

Hopefully, to tell you about a job lead.

Having business cards printed used to be fairly expensive, but now, they are within everyone's reach. Companies like Vistaprint have regular specials where you can order on-line 500 business cards for $10.00.

I have purchased from Vistaprint when they have offered special deals. 500 cards for $10.00... it's hard to beat that deal.

Some job-searching networkers struggle with the fact they don't have a business to promote and they're not sure what to put on their card as their title. I believe they tend to over think this part of the process.

If you have a professional designation, you would insert it, right after your name. A quick example would be using myself... Rae A. Stone-house R.N., if I was looking for a nursing position.

With business cards being so inexpensive and if you are searching for work in more than one field, you could easily purchase additional cards that identify you as working in those fields.

When in a networking interaction, if you have your different cards with you, you could easily produce one that connects you with a specific field of discussion.

Now you have your business or calling card, we need to look at the process of sharing your card. Despite what some people think, there is a protocol.

The Japanese take the presentation of a business card in a one to one networking situation far more serious than we do. To them, ritual is involved.

When presented with a business card you are expected to accept it with both hands, hold it in front of you and read the content of the card, both sides. You would then hold it with respect as the other person shares their elevator pitch.

You would only place it in your pocket after you had left the person and you would never deface the card by writing on it.

In North America, we are a little less respectful.

Sometimes, quite a bit!

I have met a fellow that within the first seconds of meeting him he announces "Well let's get this out of the way" and hands me his card. I expect he wasn't as comfortable or skilled at networking as he thought he was.

I have also seen an influential woman walk up to a group of people and start passing out her business cards. "Here you go, one for you and one for you!"

She then left the group and went over to another and repeated the process. It was like she was feeding chickens or passing out candy to children who were trick or treating at her door.

The purpose of passing out her business card seemed to be missed. I wonder if she was actually shy and was covering up her uncomfortableness?

So, what is the correct way to present your card to another? How and when?

I'm sure everybody has their own view on the matter.

When I have been offered another's business card as part of an introduction that is under way, I will adopt what I described earlier as the Japanese method.

I will accept it, quickly read the details and I will keep it in my hand in full view. I see the offering of a business card from another as the cue to offer mine in return.

I often make a comment about a detail or an aspect of their business card to reinforce that I have taken a serious look at it. If I don't see any action from my partner towards offering their business card, I will initiate it myself.

Asking, "Do you have a business card?" can be easier than saying "Here is my business card."

Of course, their providing a card opens it up for me to provide mine. I will also listen for a verbal cue of "I should get in contact with you", "I will keep in touch" or anything close to that as a signal for me to offer my card.

∿

IN OUR NEXT CHAPTER, WE LOOK AT SHAKING HANDS, A NECESSARY PART of networking.

8. WHOLE LOTTA SHAKING GOING ON

I've titled this chapter **Whole Lotta Shaking Going On**, because when you are out there networking, meeting new people and greeting people you already know, there *really* is a lot of handshaking going on.

A handshake is more than just a greeting. It is also a message about your personality and confidence level.

In business, a handshake is an important tool in making the right first impression. The same applies when you are job searching.

Your *business* is finding yourself a job.

Let's take a closer look at the simple act of shaking another's hand. Maybe, it's not so simple after all!

Before extending your hand, introduce yourself. Extending your hand should be part of an introduction, not a replacement for using your voice.

This isn't the cue to start reciting your elevator pitch though.

Extending your hand without saying anything may make you appear nervous or overly aggressive. On one hand (pun intended!) it would seem shaking someone's hand should be an easy process. We have likely been doing it most of our adult life.

On the other hand, some people seem to have problems with it.

I believe part of the problem that creates anxiety is we over think things sometimes. We are anxious because we give more importance to the activity than it really deserves, and it takes on a life of its own, creating anxiety.

A self-fulfilling prophesy if there ever was one.

Another part that probably creates anxiety is we can only control our portion of the interaction. If our partner is an experienced hand-shaker, then all should go smoothly but many aren't.

There are a few *different* hand-shaking styles that come up in the literature and I am sure you have likely experienced them yourselves.

I personally don't like grasping someone's hand who has the so-called 'wet fish' handshake. It can leave you with an obsessive urge to wipe your hand as soon as you can, but fight the urge.

Even worse, there are times my hand is sweating and I don't want the label. I have developed the habit of giving my hand a quick, unobtrusive wipe on my pant leg before offering my hand.

THEN THERE IS "BONE-CRUSHER BILL." THE OFFERED HAND OFTEN

comes in as a curve from the hip of Bill with the express purpose of crushing walnuts.

Or so it would seem.

Bill never seems to realize the pain he causes in others or the fact people start to avoid him. Word can get around!

Another ineffective handshake I call the "**Royal**" handshake.

Someone only offers you the tips of their fingers and no matter how you try you can't seem to grasp more than a few fingers. You are left feeling you were robbed.

The bottom line is *you* should avoid being any of these profiles. If you need to practice at home before going to a networking session, do so.

It seems to be coming more common that friends are hugging when meeting in a social setting. There are many people are what I call 'huggy' people.

I would suggest waiting to see if you offered one rather than expecting one. It could make for an awkward situation if you were to offer a hug on a first contact and it wasn't welcomed.

Maintaining Eye Contact

Closely related to hand-shaking and interacting with a new contact is that of maintaining your eye contact.

Many people have challenges maintaining eye contact with their conversational partner at the best of times. This can have different reasons.

For some cultures, it is inappropriate to look another in the eyes. Avoiding eye contact can be a sign of respect or deference to the other.

For the most part, maintaining eye contact in a conversation can demonstrate confidence. A couple challenges come to mind though.

A difference in height between the speakers can be challenging, probably more for the short person looking up than the taller person looking down.

Another challenge in a busy room is to focus on your conversational partner, not on people passing by or other conversations going on. It can distract you and give the impression you are looking for a better conversation to join. If you partner is displaying this particular behaviour, they may well be scanning the room for a better opportunity.

∽

IN OUR NEXT CHAPTER, WE EXPLORE THE IMPORTANCE OF FOLLOWING UP with what you said you were going to do.

"DEFINE YOUR GOALS IN TERMS OF THE ACTIVITIES NECESSARY TO achieve them, and concentrate on those activities." — Brian Tracy

9. FOLLOW-UP IS EVERYTHING!

It can be a great feeling when coming home from a networking event and looking at the stack of business cards you have collected. You even spoke at length to many of the card-donators.

Some, it can be a little difficult to recall who they were.

"Now was he the tall fellow with the bad hair piece... or was he...?" You've probably experienced that scenario more than once. And you know what... perhaps some business people you gave your precious business card to are thinking something similar.

Hopefully not about your bad hair though.

For effective business networking, I recommend the *quality* over *quantity* method of networking.

Some would say networking is a numbers game, the *more* you meet the *higher* the chances of your meeting someone who can benefit you.

Take for example, you are meeting someone for the first time and if the setting and conditions permit, they deliver their elevator pitch and you return with yours. Then comes the awkward moment, what to say next.

You can either carry on conversing about something of no consequence "Nice day, eh?" until one of you tires of it or you can explore common interests. Assuming, you have a common interest, I would suggest you take the lead in the conversation in getting the other to expand upon the commonality or something they had previously said.

Many networkers make the mistake of trying to sell their *product or themselves* at this juncture. Your *goal* should be to arrange to meet them at *another* time, perhaps for coffee, to discuss those common areas further.

Even though many of us are electronically connected to our offices by our smart phones and can probably check to see if we are available at a certain date and time to make a coffee date, we likely won't.

When you suggest meeting for coffee, later, if the person is willing to set up a date and time, on the spot, I would go with it. Location can always be determined later by e-mail.

If they aren't willing to set a time and date, I would refer to their business card and say something to the effect of "Can I reach you at this e-mail?

"I'll contact you next week and see if we can set up a time to get together for a quick coffee."

Unfortunately, for many networkers, this is as far as they go. They don't do the follow-up. Life gets busy, there is always one more thing to do with your business and before you know it you have lost the window of opportunity.

There is a strong possibility the individual you were networking with also has a list of people they are following up with and other commitments. It is far too easy to get left by the wayside if you don't take action to stand out from the others.

At a recent morning meeting of my Business Referral Group we discussed the issue of follow up.

A fellow member, related that in his experience, if you actually follow-up with a lead, it puts you way ahead of those who don't.

He makes a practice of following up with a networking connection within three days of the original meeting and says it is amazing how many people have said to him "You know, you are one of the few who actually follows up."

Yes, following up can help you stand out from the competition.

THE COFFEE GET-TOGETHER IS THE OPPORTUNITY FOR EACH OF YOU TO share your business or professional details and determine if there is enough reason to continue at another time to develop your relationship further and ideally to do business together.

You might ask "I've contacted them three times by e-mail and even left a couple voice mails but they haven't gotten back to me. What do I do next?"

There could be a legitimate reason for them not getting back to you. Life happens! But they could be acting non-assertively and are actively avoiding you.

I would have to respond with "If that was *true*, is that someone you *really* want to network with or to do business with?" If you are to continue, it could easily label you as a stalker.

One suggestion may be to add them to your tickler file. A tickler file is like a day-timer or a planner and you add a date and a time to follow up on a specific item.

A couple weeks down the road, ignoring the fact they haven't acknowledged you yet, you would be justified in sending them a message something like "I just noticed we didn't get together a few weeks ago like we said we would.

Where did the time go? It seems to be picking up speed.

Last time we met we were discussing our common interests of... Are you still interested in getting together?"

If you still don't receive a response, I would put them in the 'inactive' file.

When it comes to networking, to *stand out* from your competition, remember to *follow-up*.

❧

IN THE NEXT CHAPTER, WE LOOK AT SOME THINGS YOU *SHOULDN'T* DO when you are networking.

"MAKING A LIVING IS EITHER A STAIRWAY TO A COFFIN... OR A STEPPING stone to greatness... your path awaits you." — Doug Firebaugh

10. TOP 15 NETWORKING NO-NOS

Throughout this section and in articles I have written, I have provided tips & techniques to help improve networking effectiveness.

I thought it would be informative and perhaps entertaining to look at the subject from a *different* perspective i.e. what you really *shouldn't* do.

It's a good way to reinforce what you *should* do.

These aren't provided in any order of priority.

See if you recognize any of them from your adventures in networking land.

- **No Show: (Not showing up for an appointment)** When all is said and done it can be argued all you really own in life is your reputation.

There are some people who don't respect other people's time. They make appointments they don't intend to keep, or they pre-empt the appointment for something more important than meeting with you.

Soon they get the reputation of not being reliable or keeping commitments. Is this the reputation you want to develop?

- **No Follow-up: (Not following up on something you said you would do)**

BNI (Business Network International) founder Dr. Ivan Misner promotes the concept of 'givers gain.'

Offering to help someone with something or providing information can help an individual move their business forward without expecting compensation, is a good way to develop a network connection.

Not following-up on what you said you were going to do takes away from your credibility and your reputation.

- **No Follow-up: (Not following through with contacting a connection)**

If you say you are going to follow-up with someone... do so.

If you don't... at the least, you have missed an opportunity to develop a potential profitable connection. At the worst, well who knows!

See **Follow-up is Everything!** in the Resource Section for an expanded version of why you should follow-up.

- **Not focussing on your conversation partner i.e. looking around the room for a better offer.**

I THINK WE ARE ALL GUILTY OF THIS AT ONE TIME OR ANOTHER. LET'S face it, not everybody is interesting to listen to.

And you know what... our conversation partner might be thinking the same thing about us!

Listening is a skill.

You will find the more you listen to people, the more they think you are interested in them, the more they will reveal about themselves and they will think you are a fantastic conversationalist.

- **Using sexist or racist language.**

I HEAR THIS FAR TOO OFTEN IN CONVERSATIONS WITH PEOPLE WHO should know better. It isn't acceptable, and I don't want to hear it.

When you are looking for work and out there making connections, you really don't want people to remember you as a sexist or racist.

- **Fly undone!**

GENTS FOR HEAVEN'S SAKE CHECK YOUR FLY WHEN YOU LEAVE THE restroom.

It might be a great conversation starter "So the bull's ready to get out is it?" But is this where you want the conversation to go?

It can be challenging to recover from a position of embarrassment. Trust me, I know. I was on stage for two hours once as an emcee with my fly undone

- **I'm so wonderful! (Going on and on about yourself and not** giving the other person a chance to talk)

IF YOU HAVE BEEN ON THE RECEIVING END OF LISTENING TO ONE OF these types, you will know it is not fun.

I would suggest hitting the *Pause* button and move on to the next opportunity.

While you should have your own story ready to share, which includes the fact you are searching for work, you should be prepared to listen closely to the other person and learn more about them.

- Talking about someone else i.e. a third party who isn't part of the conversation in a derogatory manner.

SOME PEOPLE ARE HAPPIEST WHEN THEY ARE PUTTING SOMEBODY ELSE down.

If you participate with someone like this, you are validating their behaviour and you will likely soon be labelled the same way. This is basically gossip.

You can bet, if a gossip is telling you something juicy about someone else, they are also telling someone else about you.

Don't be a gossip!

- Dump job: (Using your conversational partner as a sounding board without asking their permission to do so)

WE ALL HAVE CHALLENGES IN LIFE, PROBLEMS THAT ARE BOTHERING US right now. It won't help your networking success rate if you become known as a whiner. That's what counsellors are for.

Leave your complaints at home and come prepared with a success-focussed story to share. You don't even have to be the hero in your story. You can tell a story about how you helped someone else become successful.

- **Monopolizing the Other Person's Time:**

THIS IS A LITTLE DIFFERENT FROM WHAT IS OUTLINED IN #7 I'M SO Wonderful!

If you are shy or uncomfortable with networking, it can be easy to stay with one person longer than you should. You are depriving both of you the opportunity to meet other people.

- **Disrespecting a Business Card:**

PEOPLE TEND TO TAKE THEIR BUSINESS CARD QUITE SERIOUSLY. IT IS AN extension of who they are.

We aren't as serious about it as say the Japanese however, picking your teeth with someone's business card is a not a great way to make friends and influence people.

- **Hit & Run: (Acting like a Shark)**

SHARKS ARE A TYPE OF NETWORKER WHO GO TO A BUSINESS NETWORKING event with the intent of making a sale right there, right now.

They don't care about you or your business. They are only interested in what they can get from you.

Don't be one! And don't allow yourself to be attacked by one either!

- **Not having Your Own Business Cards:**

THIS PORTRAYS THE IMAGE YOU ARE NOT A SERIOUS NETWORKER.

If you haven't even taken the time to develop and produce business cards to promote yourself, then why would I want to do business with you?

I have heard it said, "Oh I don't do business cards." "I take the time to write their name down on a piece of paper with their contact information."

"It's more personal, and then I contact them with, hey remember me?"

"Lame, lame, lame." That's all I can say about that comment.

I recall a speed-networking event I organized. It was very much like speed dating, except it was for the purpose of developing business connections.

One young fellow who worked as a high-end office furniture salesman didn't bring any business cards. When I asked him why he didn't bring any cards, he smiled and said "How can anybody forget this beautiful face?"

Well, I guess they did forget his beautiful face because a month or so later I saw him in his new line of work filling ice cream cones at our local Dairy Queen.

- **Eating Food While Conversing:**

Many networking events offer food & beverage.

Balancing a paper plate in one hand and a drink in the other can be challenging when reaching your hand out to shake another's hand. My personal belief is if I am eating, I will stand to the side and chow down, then when finished, I will resume networking.

I have had to stand an awfully long time with a plate of food in my hand while listening to another to avoid appearing rude.

Word to the wise... be careful of spinach dips. Spinach stuck to your teeth can take your conversational partner's focus in different directions than what you intended.

- **Networking While Inebriated:**

You are your own liquor control board. If you can't handle your liquor without getting mouthy, don't drink!

What you say and do may come back to haunt you.

❧

In the next chapter, we take another look at using LinkedIn as a job searching tool.

11. LINKEDIN REVISITED

In the last section, we briefly mentioned utilizing Linkedin as a tool to develop connections that can hopefully be a source of employment leads for you.

So how do you do so?

Let's go back to basics to answer that question.

When Linkedin was first developed, we were encouraged to upload our resumes to our Linkedin profile. If you had a long work career, your experience section included the duties and responsibilities you had taken on over the years, could be quite lengthy.

It was very much like having your resume on steroids. It seemed the more you had posted, the better.

The same applied to creating your resume. The more you had written, the better off you were.

As they say... the times are changing.

If you are brand new to the concept of Linkedin, let me keep it brief by saying that you can easily sign up for an account for free.

As I understand, people go to Linkedin for three main purposes:

- One, to look for *work* or *opportunities*.
- Two, to find someone to *hire* for their business.
- And three, they are looking for a *solution* to a problem they have.

When setting up your professional profile you need to be thinking *self-promotion*.

At this point in your life... that is being in job-search mode, you need to be *easily* seen as a solution to somebody's problem. Your solution of course is you are willing to work for them and you have the skills and expertise to do so.

The promotional copy you add to your Linkedin profile has to not only *grab* your reader's attention from the beginning, it has to *quickly* position you as someone who is worth digging deeper into your profile.

As I have said before, your Linkedin profile, starting with your name, title and summary, should be consistent with what you have written in your resume.

Your **Summary Statement** from your resume fits in quite well as the summary for your Linkedin profile.

The content you have added to the *Experience* section of your resume also fits in well to your **Linkedin Experience** section with the added benefit of being able to expand upon your personal information you weren't able to do within the limitations of a resume.

If you have any publications or examples of work you have created that would be of benefit to your job search, Linkedin is a good place to feature them.

In a previous chapter, we talked about using business cards in networking. Especially when job searching, there is value in posting your Linkedin url to your business card.

The same applies with posting your Linkedin url to your resume. You want to make it as easy as possible for people to research you and what solution you might have to offer them.

The other sections of your Linkedin profile should also be completed with a *self-promotional* slant, keeping in mind you still need to be professional.

moderately
shameless
self-promotion

Linkedin is not Facebook. Anything you post to the timeline should be professional in nature and shed you in a good light. That is, it should position you as a *credible, experienced* if not an expert, in your field.

Up to this point, we have been talking about you promoting yourself on Linkedin as part of your overall job-searching strategy. Another equally beneficial feature of Linkedin is you can search for jobs in the geographical area you want to work in by entering your search query into the Search box on your home page.

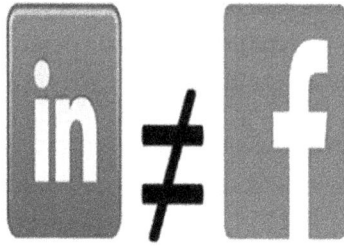

Please keep professional

In the graphic below, I clicked on the *Jobs link*, then I entered the term 'Nurse Jobs' in the screen that came up.

You can fine tune it for different geographical areas if you are considering relocating or your own area if you aren't.

Something to remember though is these are just the jobs that have been listed on Linkedin by the people who are trying to fill the vacancies. It doesn't mean this is a complete listing of jobs available. You will have to check other on-line sources.

With Linkedin, you can search for members that share similar titles as the job you are interested in applying for.

The advantage to doing so is you can look at their profile to see if there are any ideas or content that you could leverage for your profile that is to add to it.

IN THE GRAPHIC BELOW, I CLICKED ON THE *PEOPLE LINK*, THEN ENTERED *Health and Safety Specialist* as my search term.

There is value in checking out the profiles of people you have connected with on Linkedin. Perhaps they may have something posted that could be a resource to you by way of added knowledge or a connection to somebody who could forward your job-searching activities.

In addition, it is worthwhile doing a search for the company or organization you are interested in or have applied for. You can gain some interesting insights about them if they have a company Linkedin profile set up. This could be the kind of information that would help you in a job interview with them, perhaps even insider information.

To conclude ... this chapter, how to leverage Linkedin for job-searching, is easily a subject we could spend a lot of time on.

Like every other aspect of your job-searching strategies, that is developing your resumes, building a network and a team of references, it is only one piece and it has to be consistent with everything else. Make sure you take the time to develop your profile fully and start building and leveraging your connections.

Remember the concept of *Givers Gain...* a concept developed by Dr. Ivan Misner, Founder of Business Networking International. If you *give* something or a service to someone else, *without* the expectation of something in return, the odds are you will *receive* something in return.

This can be something as simple as sending an article to someone who you think might benefit from it or perhaps writing an informational article on a subject you are experienced in. And what you receive in return, doesn't necessarily come from someone who you have given to. It could be a connection of theirs or perhaps a complete stranger.

Some might call it Karma, others might call it the Law of Attraction in action. Either way, it is a good value and practice to develop.

~

IN THE NEXT SECTION, WE CREATE STRATEGIES TO MAXIMIZE YOUR references.

"WORK IS EFFORT APPLIED TOWARD SOME END. THE MOST SATISFYING work involves directing our efforts toward achieving ends that we ourselves endorse as worthy expressions of our talent and character." -- William J. Bennett

"YOU HAVE TO DO MORE THAN YOU GET PAID FOR BECAUSE THAT'S where the fortune is." -- Jim Rohn

SECTION TWO: REFERENCE STRATEGIES

12. MAXIMIZING YOUR REFERENCES

In this section, we look closely at how to strategize and use your references effectively.

The right list of personal references can be the key to success in securing follow-up interviews.

Each reference should:

- Consent to give a reference about you.

- Have a surname different from yours (even if unrelated).

- Work in an office where he or she can receive calls during business hours and can privately *tell* (rhymes with 'sell') about you intelligently, credibly, and enthusiastically.

- Be thoroughly prepared by you to give a *knowledgeable, motivational, inspirational* reference.

Additional Reference Attributes:

As you create your list of preference references, besides being a cheerleader for you as to how wonderful you are, look for these additional attributes:

- A successful professional life.

- A self-confident, upbeat, outgoing demeanour.

- Good oral and written communication skills.

- A fondness for you (with a little PR, if necessary).

- A desire, (preferably burning) to help you succeed.

Remember, you have a wide field to draw from in order to pick perfect professional references.

By only considering former supervisors or college instructors as references, most job seekers neglect 80 percent of the potential reference population.

Who could be your influential references?

Review your career history and your current business contacts for the names of influential references who can give you *search security* without *job jeopardy*. Your list might include:

- Former supervisors.

- Your boss's boss and other high-level executives at past employers who knew your contributions.

- Coworkers at present or past employers who witnessed your skills and effectiveness.

- Subordinates who can verify your management ability.

- Colleagues or others who served with you on committees or task forces.

- Members of trade associations or other professional groups who know you.

If you haven't already, generate a list of potential references that meet the above criteria.

$\backsim$

IN THE NEXT CHAPTER, WE LOOK AT MATCHING YOUR REFERENCES TO specific jobs you are applying.

13. MATCH YOUR REFERENCES TO THE TARGET JOB

O ur next step is to take the names from the lists you generated after reading the last chapter and match those references to your target job.

For each prospective position, pick a back-up team of *specialty* references.

These people have special knowledge of:

- The target company

- Influential people at the target company

- The industry in which the company is involved

- Influential people in the industry whose names can be used

- The particular skills required which you possess

LINE UP THE DEFENCE

No matter how you plan to play your references, follow protocol. (It's not just polite. It's the only way to win.)

When you intend to give a reference's name to an interviewer, or at the very least, as soon as you have, *inform* the reference of the fact!

Provide them information about:

- Who may be calling

- From what company

- About what position

~

IN THE NEXT CHAPTER, WE LOOK AT HOW YOU CAN PREPARE YOUR references for when they are called to talk about you.

"EVERYTHING COMES TO HIM WHO HUSTLES WHILE HE WAITS." -- **Thomas Edison**

"WE MUST LEARN TO APPLY ALL THAT WE KNOW SO THAT WE CAN attract all that we want." **Jim Rohn**

14. PROFESSIONAL REFERENCE QUESTIONS LIST

B efore you call upon your references to put them to work, you should help make it easier for them by providing them with a copy of the **Professional Reference Questions List** or the **Personal Reference Questions List as applicable.**

They're included in your Additional Resources Section at the end of this book.

Let's look at the one for Professional references first.

The idea behind these lists is for you to make it easier for your references to *rave* about you.

You will notice some questions are requesting some factual information from your references and others are asking for their opinion.

The idea would be to consult with your references before you go for an interview and help them fill out the form. Some might appreciate your help, others may not.

The Professional Reference Questions List

- **How long have you known?**

Hopefully, the people you have chosen for references have known you for some time.

- **How do you know?**

This question is asking your reference in what capacity do they know you.

- **Did they work alongside of you in a particular job?**

- **Did they supervise you?**

- **Did you supervise them?**

The *strength* of your reference is *increased* if they are able to demonstrate they have a good idea of how you work.

- **When was he/she hired?**

You would likely need to provide this information for your reference, especially if you are no longer working with them.

- **When did he/she leave?**

The same applies to this question.

If you no longer work with this particular reference, provide them the date you left employment with them.

- **What was his/her salary when he/she left?**

Odds are you will have to provide this as they wouldn't likely know.

- **Why did he/she leave?**

You can provide your reference with the details as to why you left, assuming you did leave of course. Your reference should rephrase your answer to this question into their own words. That is, something they would be comfortable saying.

- **Did you work with him/her directly?**

This appears to be a fairly simple question.

The Hiring Manager is basically qualifying the reference as to how well they knew you. If your reference didn't actually work closely with you, it's not really a problem if the reference is able to describe what your working relationship was.

A Hiring Manager may give more credibility to a reference who has worked *closely* with you rather than one that you had a *passing* acquaintance with.

- **Was he/she usually on time?**

Your reference may not know the answer to this one, so I would tell them to say something like "I'm not really sure about that."

"I can't say I noticed anything related to that."

It's somewhat of an evasive answer but probably better than them saying "Oh yeah, he was late all the time!" You're not going to win any points with a response like that one.

- **Was he/she absent from work very often?**

Your reference may not know the answer to this question.

If you haven't been absent from work a lot, you may want to impress upon your reference you pride yourself on being able to make it to work regularly. Likely, the Hiring Manager will want to hear something like that.

If you have been absent from work quite a bit recently and over the not so distant past, you may want to come up with some kind of explanation as to why you were sick. Your personal health is confidential and of nobody else's business, however a sick time record can work against you when it comes to getting hired.

- **Did his/her personal life ever interfere with his/her work?**

Whoever is checking out your references shouldn't likely be able to ask this question, but don't be surprised if they do. The best answer would be "No, not that I am aware of."

- **What were his/her titles?**

This is a simple question to identify what your job title was. Make sure your reference is matched with the particular job title you had at the time.

The Hiring Manager is also likely checking up on you to see if the job title you actually had, is the same as the one you have identified in your resume.

- **What were his/her duties?**

You may have to explain them to your reference.

If they were had the same job duties as you, they would obviously know them. Others may not though.

The challenge here is that your reference may not have a clear understanding of what your duties were. If you provide them a list and they just read the list off, it's not going to look very good for you.

Another consideration is the Hiring Manager when contacting your references, may want to dig a little deeper about what you have written on your resume. If your reference has an in-depth knowledge of you and your job duties, then well great. If not, your reference might be better off coming up with an evasive answer.

- **Did he/she cooperate with supervisors?**

This is a loaded question.

The desired answer would be "*of course!*"

- **Did he/she cooperate with co-workers?**

This leads to a similar answer as above. You will want to make it seem that you get along well with everyone.

- **Did he/she take work home very often?**

It's hard to say how to answer this one.

On one hand, bringing work home can look like you are a *dedicated, diligent worker*, willing to go the extra step to get something done.

On the other hand, bringing work home could indicate you have a problem with completing your work during your working hours. It could also indicate a worker is having work vs home issues.

You could appear to be *out of balance* if you are doing *work at work* and *work at home*.

- **What are his/her primary attributes?**

This leads to a subjective answer from your references. They will have to come up with their own answer.

Hopefully it will be a glowing, positive one about you.

- **What are his/her primary liabilities?**

This is similar to the last one. They will have to come up with their own answer.

The problem is that this might work against you, so it might be wise to offer a rather small liability but illustrate how you are *currently* resolving it.

So, what you are doing is turning a **weakness** into a **strength**. You'll have to share this with your reference of course.

- **Is he/she eligible for rehire?** If your reference is a co-worker, they wouldn't likely be able to answer this. But if your reference is your manager, they would likely know.

Let's hope they say yes. Otherwise, you should probably be looking for another reference.

Can you confirm the information he/she has given?

Your reference will have to wait and see what they are asked.

∾

IN THE NEXT CHAPTER, WE LOOK AT A *PERSONAL REFERENCE QUESTIONS List*, for friends and colleagues.

.   .   .

"DON'T SAY, "IF I COULD, I WOULD." SAY, "IF I CAN, I WILL." —
Jim Rohn

15. PERSONAL REFERENCE QUESTIONS LIST

This list is one you will use for references that are more of the *personal* nature.

These are friends or perhaps people who you have worked with in a voluntary capacity. They would have a good idea of what you are like, outside of work and would do a good job of referring you.

While it is helpful these references know what job it is you are applying for and what your background is that makes you believe that you can do the job, they *don't* need an *in depth* understanding of the job.

They just need to be able to talk about how it was working alongside of you. They also need to be able to speak concisely and clear. You don't want somebody as a referral who gets tongue-tied under pressure.

THE PERSONAL REFERENCE QUESTIONS LIST

- **How long have you known?**

Make sure your reference has an answer for this question.

A long-winded "well let me see. My son was three at the time and now he's eight. But wait a minute… my daughter was two when we met. I remember him coming to her birthday party. No… wait that can't be right!"

Their answer should be *short and sweet*.

- **How do you know?**

You and your reference need to agree where it was you met.

Did you work together on a volunteer project or serve on a non-profit board of directors?

- **What is your opinion of?**

This is a subjective answer on the part of your reference of course.

Hopefully, they think highly of you and do some cheerleading on your behalf as part of their response to the question.

- **Does he/she get along well with others?**

As in the previous questions for your professional references, you want your answer to be "yes, you do!"

- **Is he/she usually on time?**

Your personal reference may not know how to answer this one.

- **Is he/she absent from work very often?**

The same as the previous question, they may not know anything about your working conditions.

- **Does he/she bring work home very often?**

Probably best to answer "I don't really know."

- **Does he/she like his/her job?**

If you are currently employed and looking for another job, it would be worthwhile for your personal reference to understand of course you like your current job, but you are looking to improve yourself through a job change.

You wouldn't want them saying you don't like your job or hate it as it won't help your case at all.

- **What are his/her primary attributes?**

They can prepare for this question on their own.

- **What are his/her primary liabilities?**

Encourage your reference to come up with something mild.

This isn't the time to draw attention to your major short-comings. There is nothing wrong with having them, we all do. But the Hiring Manager doesn't need to know them at this point.

❧

In the next chapter, we look at strategies to be proactive in your job searching and put your references to work, even before they are called by an employer checking up on you.

16. GO ON THE OFFENCE

You needn't wait for your employers to call before you put your references into the game.

Those specialized *preference references* can write or phone the prospect to give your prospects a boost.

Here's how.

Letters That Lock in the Target

A *second*, post-interview letter *must* be:

A *super-reference*, written by the *right* person, targeted to the *right* person (*a decision maker*), and containing marketable information about your abilities and skills.

What someone *says* about you has *ten times* the influence of what you say about yourself.

Use a *brief*, perfectly drafted one-page letter from a *carefully* selected reference as a cover letter for your resume.

Personalize each letter to individuals inside the target company(ies) who either have:

The *authority* to hire you, or

Connections to those who do.

The key is positioning.

The *position* of your reference, the way you are *positioned* by your reference in a letter or telephone call, targeting a *specific* position, and someone in a *position* to hire for it, are all essential elements of a super-reference.

To position yourself for the perfect position, choose a reference who is the best position to write the best positioning letter for you.

Who Should Write?

Selection of the reference cover letter writer is the first element of positioning.

He or she should be:

- Someone who knows the recipient of the letter

- Someone who knows someone else the recipient knows

- Someone who, by reputation, is known to the recipient of the letter

- Someone whose letterhead, title, and responsibilities will attract the recipient's attention or give *credibility* to the statements in the letter --- and to you

Help Them Say the Right Thing

Most references simply don't have a clue when it comes to writing the perfect letter.

That's why typical reference letters are ridiculous. References aren't particularly good learners, either. After all, if they weren't more important than you, you wouldn't need them to lend you their importance, right?

It's not only their belief --- it's yours.

So rather than try to teach them or leave the letters' impact to chance, write your *perfect* letters *yourself*! The result is a far more detailed, consistent presentation, and your references will probably be relieved.

Just ask. You'll probably hear: "Sure, whatever you want. Just type it up and I'll sign it."

If the reference is a personal friend or colleague well known to the target, the opening and closing paragraphs should be in the writer's own words. But you can help by supplying the language for the *value* paragraph.

When you let your references know of the impending reference check, let them in on your excitement too. Fill your reference in on what you've learned from the interview and what kind of call he or she can expect, from what kind of person.

Don't coach your references so well they sound 'canned,' but do be sure each one understands:

The objectives of your job search

The specific knowledge you'd like him or her to relate in a reference call

The delivery necessary for maximum impact on the reference checker

Ask your references to accept the telephone calls or return them immediately (you'll pay any toll charges), and to notify you of the details the moment they hang up. You need the feedback and you need it fast.

Always re-contact your references after they've made their play in your behalf to:

Express your gratitude and appreciation

Ask about their impression of your prospective employer --- and your prospects

Express your gratitude and appreciation. Again.

∞

"BE YOURSELF; NO BASE IMITATOR OF ANOTHER, BUT YOUR BEST SELF. There is something which you can do better than another. Listen to the inward voice and bravely obey that. Do the things at which you are great, not what you were never made for." — Ralph Waldo Emerson

SECTION THREE: ADDITIONAL RESOURCES

Here is a collection of job interview preparation related questions asked on Quora.com and answered by me, Rae Stonehouse.

It's cumbersome to add hyperlinks in this printed version, so I haven't.

If you would like to read more answers to the questions, from people who may or may not agree with me... and some... who may be from outer space and worth a chuckle, just visit Quora and enter the title of the question into their search bar.

~

17. QUESTION: WHAT ARE THE CHALLENGES OF WRITING A LINKEDIN PROFILE?

Answer Provided:

The question asks what are the *challenges* of writing a Linkedin profile.

Challenges are relative to the person creating their own Linkedin profile.

It may depend on several factors:

- You need to have a high level of literacy. Any spelling mistakes or grammatical errors you make will work against you.

- You need to have good strategic thinking skills. We all likely have a long list of jobs, skills and/or accomplishments we could post. But should we? Your Linkedin profile has to be consistent with your purpose of creating it in the first place. Sometimes, less is more.

- You need to get comfortable with promoting yourself. As a business would when marketing itself, your Linkedin profile is marketing you. You have to make sure it is written to present you in the best possible light.

- It's no longer a matter of sharing what you have done in the past, it's a matter of promoting what you can do in the future. You need to craft your content so it comes across as a solution to somebody else's problem.

- You need to get comfortable with writing about yourself in the 3rd person vs 1st person 'I' statements.

- If you are searching for work, your Linkedin profile has to be consistent with your resume. Your Linkedin profile allows you to expand upon some of the claims you have made on your resume and provide examples of your work.

- You need to fill out all of the areas in your profile. This not only means filling in dates and titles, it means providing content once again, shows you in a good light.

- You need to actively build your network of connections. Consider 500 connections as a minimum. It may be the first thing many people look at. If your connections number is low, some may wonder if it's worthwhile connecting to you.

Linkedin is one of many social media venues. You need to ensure your digital footprint is consistent with the professional image you want to portray.

You should consider your Linkedin profile as being iterative. It needs to be tweaked and adapted on an ongoing basis.

If you are using it for job searching, you may want to keep a file of different content e.g. jobs and duties you have had in the past and then change your Linkedin profile whenever you are applying for a job.

From my perspective, there are at least two categories of connections on Linkedin. There are those that take a lackadaisical approach to connecting and those who take it very seriously.

Linkedin is merely a tool for you to use to promote yourself. At present, it is likely the best one for achieving results.

As originally answered on Quora.com.

∾

"AN AFFIRMATION IS SIMPLY A POSITIVE DECLARATION OF SOMETHING you believe to be true or something you expect to become true and desire to live by. Affirmations transform your thinking, your attitudes, and finally, your behavior. Their impact on attitudes and behavior help to produce the results you desire." — Paul J Meyer

"WHATEVER YOU BELIEVE WITH EMOTION BECOMES REALITY. YOU always act in a manner consistent with your innermost beliefs and convictions." — Brian Tracy

"THERE IS NO REASON TO EVER QUIT... UNLESS OF COURSE YOU HAD NO plans to ever succeed... that is called 'Delusional Success' "— Doug Firebaugh

18. QUESTION: HOW AM I SUPPOSED TO NETWORK IF I AM SHY AND SOCIALLY ANXIOUS AND AVOID SOCIAL EVENTS?

Answer Provided:

Well, the good news, if there is any, is you are not alone. I don't know where in the world you are located but the Shyness Institute, located in the USA, reports that more than 50% of North Americans describe themselves as being shy in social situations.

You would think with all this social media and on-line connectedness, we would be becoming more social and less shy, but the opposite is true. This collective increase in our shyness has been attributed to several causes.

Going back to the 1950s, the invention of TV dinners may have been the start of it. Families were no longer sitting together for their evening meals and sharing the events of their day. Conversational skills started to decline. As the years and decades have passed, there has been a further erosion in families spending quality time together in what was considered a traditional family dinner. Families nowadays come in all different styles and there really isn't anything traditional at all. Many children have been deprived of opportunity to develop their conversational skills historically provided at shared family meals.

Along comes the invention of the Sony Walkman. We were able to listen to our tunes on our earphones and didn't have to listen to anyone else. ATM (automatic teller machines) have been considered another step in the increase of our shyness. We no longer have to stand in line to do our banking. That means we no longer talk to other people in the line or the teller. The same applies to many stores. We do self-checkout and don't have to have social conversation anymore, if we choose not to.

Technology developed from Walkmans to Discmans and now to smartphones that can store a phenomenal amount of music. One only has to look at a bus stop to see a dozen or so people intently looking at their smart phones, earbuds in place, frantically trying to avoid making eye contact with anyone else. It's sad, but it seems to be our new reality. If we let it!

The thing about shyness is we all experience it differently. Simply put, shyness is a lack of self-confidence and skills to use in a social situation. Nothing more... nothing less. It doesn't mean you are a bad person or a loser. It just means you haven't yet developed your skills in this area.

Unless one experiences shyness them self, I don't think they can truly appreciate how debilitating it can be. I think the advice of "suck it up buttercup" is worthless and insensitive.

Many people have conquered shyness and you can too It will take a lot of work though. I have been fighting it all my life. I consider it a life-long journey of conquering shyness. I've researched shyness, I've studied it, I've wrote about it and I speak about it. Some days I am fearless, some days my shyness will get the better of me and I will avoid attending an event.

I too have challenges with shyness preventing me from being effective in business networking. Networking is something you have to do if you want to stay in business. I've heard it said, that if you are not networking ... you are not working! I believe it to be true. And you also have to be networking all the time.

As part of my own self-directed cure for shyness and self-confidence in business networking I researched and wrote a book entitled **Power Networking for Shy People: Tips & Techniques for Moving From Shy to Sly!**

http://powernetworkingforshypeople.ca

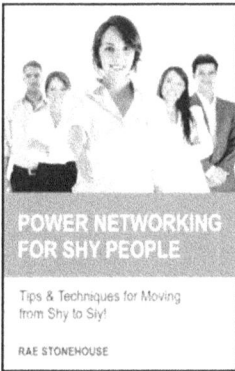

Throughout the book I provide a series of strategies to level the playing field for shy people, helping them become effective networkers. I believe you can still be shy and be an effective networker. I believe the quality of the networking encounters is more important than the quantity as some would have you believe.

Conquering a fear of any subject, with mastery of the subject in mind, is merely a matter of taking a series of small steps towards the goal. Actually have a plan in writing, with a series of steps leading towards achieving the goal, is even better.

I don't think any contributor here on Quora is able to give you a definitive answer as to how you can overcome shyness and become an effective business networker in the limited amount of space we have for our answers. I suggest purchasing my book as it is available as an inexpensive, immediately downloadable e-book. You can start your journey from shyness to self-confidence today!

As answered on Quora.com.

~

19. QUESTION: WHO'RE BEST BUSINESS NETWORKING PROFESSIONALS?

Answer Provided:

Simply answered, the best business networking professionals are those that network professionally.

Being an effective business networker involves quite a few of what might be considered soft skills. Good conversation skills, empathy, listening skills and a genuine interest to help others are a few that readily come to mind.

In attending any business networking event you can expect to see certain professions 'working the room', at least in my experience. Financial planners, realtors and insurance agents readily come to mind.

Some are effective networkers i.e. building contacts and connecting other businesses. Some are like sharks, they expect to make a kill i.e. sale, at the networking event. Those ones give everyone else a bad reputation.

Being a successful business networker involves utilizing strategies that work towards mutual benefits. Sometimes networking is like gardening. You plant seeds. You nurture them. Then with loving care, they grow to fruition.

Networking and building relationships takes time.

As answered on Quora.com.

~

"THE BIGGEST MENTAL ROADBLOCKS THAT YOU WILL EVER HAVE TO overcome are those represented by your self-limiting beliefs." — Brian Tracy

"MORALE AND ATTITUDE ARE THE FUNDAMENTAL INGREDIENTS TO success." — Bud Wilkinson

"SOME THINGS YOU HAVE TO DO EVERY DAY. EATING SEVEN APPLES ON Saturday night instead of one a day just isn't going to get the job done." — Jim Rohn

"DON'T BE AFRAID TO GIVE YOUR BEST TO WHAT SEEMINGLY ARE SMALL jobs. Every time you conquer one it makes you that much stronger. If you do the little jobs well, the big ones tend to take care of themselves."— Dale Carnegie

20. QUESTION: HOW DO I EXPAND MY PROFESSIONAL NETWORK IN COLLEGE?

Answer Provided:

My first suggestion would be to take the word 'college' out of the equation. You may be currently attending college, but that is only one aspect of the potential network you have to connect with.

Don't discount the value of networking with family, friends, neighbours, businesses and community resources that you frequent. Potential connections are all around us if we keep our eyes open to opportunity.

One of the challenges that I see with networking in colleges, universities etc. is that many of the students don't see the value of networking. They may not have any experience in the art of networking or they may be just too focussed on their studies.

This may mean that one of your first tasks in networking would be to educate the other person on the value and benefits of networking.

There are several skills involved in networking with professionals. One of them is to have your 'spidey sense' on high alert to potential people to connect with.

Combining your awareness with a tool such as Linkedin to organize can help build your network of connections. If you haven't already, create a professional profile on Linkedin. This isn't like a Facebook presence, so avoid any partying pics that you would regret posting.

After you meet someone at a social mixer of some sort, follow up with them by sending them an invite to join your professional network on Linkedin and in the real world.

Speaking of social mixers, I would suggest researching what clubs or social groups exist within the college structure that would provide you opportunity to socialize and network. Clubs like Toastmasters can be a great way to hone your speaking skills, build your self-confidence and network with like-minded individuals.

Don't rule out connecting with your instructors/professors.

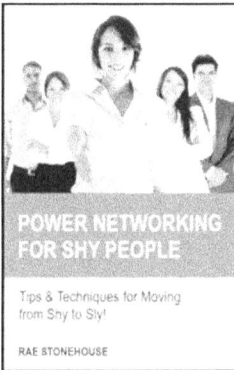

POWER NETWORKING FOR SHY PEOPLE

Tips & Techniques for Moving from Shy to Sly!

RAE STONEHOUSE

I go into quite a bit more detail in a downloadable e-book that I wrote. **Power Networking for Shy People: Tips & Techniques for Moving from Shy to Sly!** outlines strategies for effective networking whether you are shy or not.

http://powernetworkingforshypeople.ca

Good luck with building your network!

As answered on Quora.com.

∽

"THE PATH TO SUCCESS IS TO TAKE MASSIVE, DETERMINED ACTION." — **Anthony Robbins**

"ONE OF THE MARKS OF SUPERIOR PEOPLE IS THAT THEY ARE ACTION-**oriented. One of the marks of average people is that they are talk-oriented." — Brian Tracy**

21. QUESTION: WHAT ARE THE BENEFITS OF LIKE-MINDED CONNECTIONS?

A nswer Provided:

IT MIGHT BE HELPFUL TO THINK IN TERMS OF THE MUTUAL BENEFITS OF like-minded connections. While being like-minded, some may call it resonating, certainly makes it easier to communicate your desire to the other person, there is great value in offering something in return.

Being like-minded doesn't mean that they are exactly the same as you. We all have our own life-experiences, wants, desires, hopes, prejudices and biases. Even though we are like-minded on specific topics, we are still quite different.

Far too many people in business have the idea that they need to get something from somebody, whether at a cost or free. A different approach, as promoted by Dr. Ivan Misner of BNI (Business Networking International) is that of 'givers gain.' The concept simply put, is that if you give freely to others, you will receive something of equal or greater value in return.

If you are a Law of Attraction believer the concept is that if you do something favourable for somebody else, without the expectation of return from them, the Universe will see to it that you receive something in return. The challenge is in recognizing the fact that what you receive in return may not come from the person you gave to. It could come from another source.

In developing an effective business network, like-minded connections compose only one segment for you. Don't rule out connections just because you haven't established commonalities as of yet.

Thanks for the question!

As answered on Quora.com.

"ALWAYS BE EAGER TO LEARN, NO MATTER HOW SUCCESSFUL YOU MIGHT already be. In the Millionaires' Club, we sometimes invite a billionaire to come talk to us. He says, 'You're doing okay, but come on. How about if you really poured it on!'" — Jim Rohn

"ACHIEVEMENT REQUIRES MORE THAN A VISION - IT TAKES COURAGE, resolve and tenacity." — Neil Eskelin

"DON'T GET COMPLACENT. PUSH YOURSELF OUT OF YOU COMFORT ZONE and set higher standards of achievement for yourself. Once you've achieved a standard of excellence, never let it rest --- push yourself even higher."— Dave Anderson

"DARE TO GO FORWARD! HAVE YOU EVER TRIED PUSHING A STRING?" — Brian Tracy

22. QUESTION: WHAT ARE THE BEST WAYS TO NETWORK AT A BUSINESS DINNER AND LEAVE A GOOD IMPRESSION?

A nswer Provided:

Business dinners can be challenging to network at.

There are basically three elements to the event: 1) Pre-meal 2) The meal 3) Post-meal.

1) **Pre-meal:** This is the part where people are coming together. Some are standing around talking to each other, reacquainting themselves with people they already know. It can be challenging to join a group of people if you don't know any of them and introducing yourself to the group. Others may already be sitting at table and talking among themselves. You have the option of sitting at a table of strangers or with people you know. There can be advantages to either option.

You will often find people standing alone. There are shy introverts in every group. They may be waiting for someone to take the initiative to introduce themselves to them. Go for it!

2) **During the meal:** How effective you are in networking here can be limited by how the table is set up. In table rounds of 8 or 10, i.e. standard hotel options, you tend to be limited to the person on your right-

hand side and/or on your left-hand side. Cross table conversation can be challenging, however group conversations tend to be easier.

If you don't know anybody at the table and/or nobody else has taken the lead, suggest to everybody to go around the table to provide a self-introduction. This is a good opportunity to give an abbreviated elevator pitch and to pass your business cards around the table.

Long, two-sided tables, present similar challenges for conversing, in that you are limited to talking to those immediately to your left and your right. As well, depending on the width of the table, to the two or three sitting directly across from you. Once again, your business card and short elevator pitch will be put to use.

3) **Post-meal:** Sometimes people will linger about after the meal which gives you a chance to network. However, more often than naught, people want to get going on their way to other activities. Many may uncomfortable with networking, so don't stick around.

As for the best way to network, basic networking skills come into play. You only have a limited amount of time, so you need to have a plan.

In advance, learn who is attending the event that it would be worth your while to meet. If you see people you know, reacquaint yourself... find out what is new with them. And don't forget to share what is new with you. In addition, when talking to somebody you know, ask them if there is somebody at the event they know, that might be beneficial for you to meet. Then ask them to introduce you.

As in any networking event, you are collecting leads as to possible connections. When talking to someone look for common interests. If so, invite them out for coffee. Get their business card and contact them after the event to confirm the details.

Take advantage of your collection of business cards and send them an invitation to join your professional network on Linkedin.

As originally answered on Quora.com.

23. QUESTION: WHY ON LINKEDIN HAS BOASTING ABOUT ONESELF AND ONE'S ACHIEVEMENTS BECOME ACCEPTABLE AND APPLAUDED? DOES BRAGGING OR HUMILITY SERVE SOCIETY BETTER?

Answer Provided:

You ask two separate questions. Addressing the first one "Why on LinkedIn has boasting about oneself and one's achievements become acceptable and applauded?"

I'll break my response further down. You are asserting that people are 'boasting' about themselves. I don't necessarily agree with that statement.

Sure, with the sheer numbers of Linkedin members, there would have to be those that are boasting about their accomplishments. They likely do it in other aspects of their lives, be it on-line, or in person.

Linkedin has developed into a platform that allows the member to 'market' themselves.

I find that many people have a challenge with the concept of self-promotion. My perspective is North American. I realize that different cultures may have different views on self-promotion or talking about one's accomplishments.

I'm fond of a quote from Walt Whitman, American Cowboy Poet. He said that 'if you have done it… it ain't bragging!'

Creating promotional copy in your Linkedin profile that promotes you as a solution to somebody else's problem takes skill. You want to get the message across, featuring your skills, without coming across as bragging/boasting. This can be challenging if you have a lot of things on the go and desirable skills.

Is it becoming acceptable and applauded? It would answer that question by saying that it has become expected and an effective tool for promoting one's self.

If a person is searching for work, they would be well-advised to have an effective Linkedin profile that resonates with their resume. You can almost guarantee that an employer will take a look at your Linkedin profile before inviting you in for an interview, as part of their screening process.

I'm not so sure about the applauded part of the question. If your Linkedin profile doesn't reveal much about you, your requests for invitations to connect might be on the lean side.

I personally don't connect with Linkedin invitations that don't have a headshot photo, don't have any information about themselves or LIONS (Linkedin Open Networkers).

You ask '**Does bragging or humility serve society better?**'

Personally, I don't think either does. But then again, why should it require an either/or response?

I believe that there is an appropriate time to promote yourself and there are times that humility is more appropriate.

I find inspiration in 'everyday heroes.' These are people that have undertaken acts of bravery or courageous ones and when asked about it, reply with something like "I just did what needed to be done."

As answered on Quora.com.

24. QUESTION: WHAT ARE TIPS AND TRICKS TO INCREASE YOUR ODDS OF GETTING A JOB AT A COMPANY BY USING NETWORKING SKILLS?

A nswer Provided:

I would suggest utilizing a multi-faceted approach.

Firstly, research the company on-line. Locate and read their social media properties. More than likely they will have a Facebook business page, a Linkedin Business page and possibly a Twitter profile.

Find out what is important to the company. What do they believe in? What is important to them? What are they most proud of?

Secondly, find out who the key people behind the company are. What roles do they take on in the company? Then check out their individual profiles on Linkedin.

If you are comfortable in doing so, send them an invitation to connect on Linkedin and provide them with a reason that they might want to connect. Not the fact that you are looking for a job though.

If the company's social media properties allow for posting comments, see how you can add value by posting replies to their postings.

Networking face-to-face with people in hiring positions in companies can be a little tricky, in that in most cases, their networking is restricted to events that with other members of the company.

There can be benefit in leveraging your connections to see if anybody knows anyone working at the company in question, or if they have any connections there.

If you are gutsy, you may want to contact somebody in the company for an informational chat, where you ask for the opportunity to pick their brain.

In business networking events, it can be helpful to ask people you connect with out right "Do you know anybody that works at ....?

I go into strategies such as these in greater detail in my book on job search strategies that work.

As originally answered on Quora.com.

～

25. QUESTION: SHOULD YOU SMILE ON YOUR LINKEDIN PROFILE?

Answer Provided:

To start with, I'm going to assume you are referring to your Linkedin profile photo.

Smiling is usually good. However, there is a degree of smiling that seems to be generally acceptable.

People do judge a book by its cover as the saying goes. They will make a snap judgement on you based on your headshot photo.

You want to appear to be professional. People usually respond favorably when they see someone smiling. It helps them to warm up to the individual. Smiling seems to help build credibility, at least when they are speaking to a group.

I am led to believe from a Russian colleague that if a fellow Russian was smiling, the automatic response would be "I wonder what they are hiding?"

While smiling would seem appropriate, what about a picture where the individual is laughing? Perhaps if you were in the entertainment industry, it might be appropriate. Not so much I would expect for a Funeral Director or maybe even a Banker.

In a less literal perspective of smiling, I believe our promotional content should be written from a smiling perspective. I have read copy and have said to myself "This person must have been angry when they wrote it."

So, I say, have fun with your Linkedin profile and let your smile shine through your headshot photo and your promotional copy.

As originally answered on quora.com.

∾

"WE WILL RECEIVE NOT WHAT WE IDLY WISH FOR BUT WHAT WE JUSTLY earn. Our rewards will always be in exact proportion to our service." — Earl Nightingale

"DO NOT SUPPOSE THAT, IF YOU FIND SOMETHING HARD TO ACHIEVE, IT is beyond human capacity; rather, if something is possible and appropriate for man, assume that it must also be within your own reach." — Marcus Aurelius, 'The Meditations'

"IDENTIFY AND DEVELOP YOUR UNIQUE TALENTS AND ABILITIES, THE things that make you special." — Brian Tracy

26. QUESTION: DO YOU ACCEPT CONNECTION INVITATIONS FROM STRANGERS ON LINKEDIN? WHY OR WHY NOT?

Answer Provided:

I evaluate every invitation I get to connect. The first criteria I look for is 'do I actually know the person?'

If not, the second criteria is 'are they connected to one of my connections?'

Failing those two, I look to see if we share any common interests.

If they pique my curiosity, I will often connect with them. If I don't see any possible connection or I foresee a barrage of spam from my 'new best friend', I will decline the invite.

I suspect many of the invitations to connect we receive have been instigated by the Linkedin system posting it on the other person's account as someone they might want to connect with.

I often wonder about invites to connect I get from strangers who only have single digit connections and we have nothing in common.

Networking opportunities can certainly be enhanced by leveraging your Linkedin connections however, having potential receptors for any content you are trying to promote through your network can be beneficial.

I've never worried about being watched by 'malicious' people. If they truly are malicious, I have a large enough digital footprint that they could easily find ammo somewhere else besides Linkedin.

As originally answered on Quora.com.

~

"WHATEVER YOUR TALENT IS, YOU SHOULD CRAFT IT, NOURISH IT AND build on it. It is the 'niche talent' that will take you to the top of your field." — Mark Victor Hansen

START BY DOING WHAT'S NECESSARY; THEN DO WHAT'S POSSIBLE; AND suddenly you are doing the impossible. — St. Francis of Assisi

"What would you do if you knew you couldn't fail?"— Robert Schuller

"NO ONE LIMITS YOUR GROWTH BUT YOU. IF YOU WANT TO EARN MORE, learn more. That means you'll work harder for a while; that means you'll work longer for a while. But you'll be paid for your extra effort with enhanced earnings down the road." — Tom Hopkins

27. QUESTION: "IT'S NOT WHAT YOU KNOW... IT'S WHO YOU KNOW". IS NETWORKING MORE IMPORTANT THAN EDUCATION, AS NETWORKING SAVES THE LONG, LEARNING PROCESS 'TILL LATER?

Answer Provided:

I would challenge your opening statement. I don't believe that "It's not what you know. it's who you know" to be true.

I BELIEVE "IT'S NOT WHAT YOU KNOW OR WHO YOU KNOW... BUT WHO knows you know!" to be more apt.

From a personal and/or business promotion perspective, it is important to become a content expert i.e. the 'go to person' among your web of connections. You need to tell them what you know. This can be challenging of course. You don't want to come across as being a braggart.

Networking and earning an education are two separate, yet interconnected activities. Both have their merits. One shouldn't be sacrificed at the expense of others.

I don't believe there is evidence supporting your assertion that 'networking saves the long, learning process 'till later?' I think you may actually be referring to the process of mentoring.

An effective mentorship, with somebody who can show you the ropes, so to speak, can speed up the process and help flatten your learning curve.

A mentor can help you with your education. Sage advice can be every bit as important as academic filler.

Networking, on the other hand, can expose you to people who may be able to mentor you in many different areas. It takes cultivating the relationship, bearing in mind the Mentor has to get something out of the relationship from the mentee as well.

As answered on Quora.com.

~

"EVERYTHING YOU WANT IS JUST OUTSIDE YOUR COMFORT ZONE." —
Robert Allen

"ONE OF THE GREATEST SURPRISES YOU'LL EXPERIENCE IS WHEN YOU discover that you can do what you were afraid you couldn't do. Your obstacles will melt away, if instead of cowering before them, you make up your mind to walk boldly through them." — Max Steingart

"THE ONLY REAL LIMITATION ON YOUR ABILITIES IS THE LEVEL OF YOUR desires. If you want it badly enough, there are no limits on what you can achieve." — Brian Tracy

28. QUESTION: HOW SHOULD YOU INTRODUCE YOURSELF IN A WAY THAT'LL MAKE PEOPLE CARE WHO YOU ARE?

Answer Provided:

I'm going to start off in a negative fashion. I don't think it is important you spend your time on ways to introduce yourself to people, so they care. You can't force them to do so.

I believe it's far more important to introduce yourself in a manner that piques the other person's curiosity, so they want to learn more about you.

People will only care who you are when they feel you are not a threat to them or they find they share common interests with you.

This is where crafting a good elevator pitch comes in. I also believe you should have multiple elevator pitches practiced so you can use an appropriate one at any given time.

Here is an excerpt from my book Power Networking for Shy People: Tips & Techniques for Moving from Shy to Sly!

http://powernetworkingforshypeople.ca

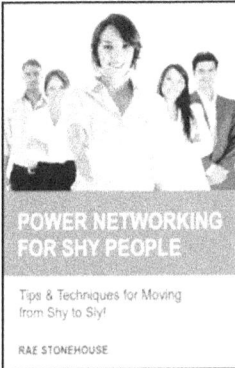

POWER NETWORKING
FOR SHY PEOPLE

Tips & Techniques for Moving
from Shy to Sly!

RAE STONEHOUSE

~

DEVELOPING YOUR ELEVATOR PITCH:

You need to develop your elevator pitch like you would a formal presentation. Just because you are introducing yourself conversationally in a 1 to 1 or a small group doesn't mean you should wing it.

Preparation is the key to your success. Rememberyou should be prepared for different lengths of elevator rides and different situations.

Follow these steps to develop your unique pitch.

Describe yourself as a solution to a problem:

The most important part of your elevator pitch is your opening sentence. You need to grab your audience's attention by telling what is unique about what you do.

In your very first sentence you need to say your name, your business' name and describe yourself as a solution to the problems your clients, customers or business associates face. Listeners don't usually care about your job title as much as what you can do for them.

When creating the first line of your elevator pitch, put yourself in the audience's shoes and answer the age-old question "What's in it for me?"

A superior elevator pitch increases your heart rate. It speaks to who you really are and what excites you about your business. If you don't get excited about it, who will?

Your pitch needs to address the five Ws.

The first step is to develop answers to the following questions:

1. What does your business do? (For example, begin your answer with "We provide.")
2. Whom does your business do it for? (For example, begin your answer with "For small and midsized healthcare providers.")
3. Why do they care? Or, What's in it for them? (For example, include in your answer "so they can ...," "who can no longer afford ...," or "who are tired of ...")
4. Why is your business different? (For example, begin your answer with "As opposed to ..." or "Unlike...")
5. What is your business? (For example, begin your answer with "My business is an insurance against ...")

Don't forget to include your **USP**, your hook. It is a good way to close off your elevator pitch. For example, using my business... Mr. Emcee Your Okanagan Event Planner of Choice. From start to finish... we do it all!

$\approx$

YOU MAY NOT BE IN BUSINESS HOWEVER THE ELEVATOR PITCH IDEA IS still a good one to facilitate introducing yourself to someone new.

As answered on Quora.com.

29. QUESTION: HOW CAN I GET OVER MY EXTREME FEAR OF TALKING TO NEW PEOPLE?

Answer Provided:

Sounds like you are caught up in what's called a 'self-fulfilling prophesy."

You expect to be afraid of talking to new people, therefore you will act in that way.

First jobs are often identified as opportunities to develop one's social skills, reduce one's shyness and build confidence. As you journey through life, every job you take on from the very first one will add to your skills and experience.

Don't let your current fear prevent you from taking on your first job. FEAR is often defined as False Expectations Appearing Real. They aren't real! We make them that way.

The only way to conquer a fear is to hit it head on and not let it control you.

I've been fearful of many things throughout my life. I was terrified of public speaking. I got tired of being afraid and decided to do something about it. Now I speak regularly and teach others how to public speak.

Your first job, which sounds like it will be an entry level, customer service one, will present you with challenges to overcome. Just because you are currently afraid, doesn't mean you will continue to be. You may open a whole set of opportunities that could lead to a career path.

You never know what will happen when you conquer a fear. A common response to conquering a fear is in wondering why it was so over-powering in the first place.

Go for it!

As answered on Quora.com.

 ∽

"IF WE DID WHAT WE ARE CAPABLE OF DOING, WE WOULD ASTOUND ourselves." — Thomas Edison

"NOTHING SPLENDID HAS EVER BEEN ACHIEVED EXCEPT BY THOSE WHO dared believe that something was superior to circumstances." author and advertising executive Bruce Barton

30. QUESTION: WHAT DO YOU TALK ABOUT OVER COFFEE?

When meeting someone for coffee professionally, what do you talk about or try to accomplish? (Particularly if you are in academia and not business)?

Answer Provided:

THERE IS LIKELY A LOT LESS DIFFERENCE BETWEEN GOING FOR COFFEE whether you are in academia or business, then you think there is. Your approach should be professional in either instance.

Going for coffee is an opportunity to get to know the other person. The objective is to find if you share common interests and if there is any opportunity to collaborate on a project or serve as a resource for each other. If you were in business, it may lead to a joint venture.

Come prepared to talk about subjects that interest you, both in your career and your private life.

I've been on a lot of 'coffee chats.' A lot of business is conducted in local coffee shops in my community.

From my personal experience, plan for 60 minutes for your coffee meeting. I find in that time both of you should have a better understanding of each other. If you resonate with each other, plan for a follow-up coffee meeting.

At the 75 to 90-minute marks, I find the conversation tending to drag and get uncomfortable.

If you want to be considered an exceptional conversationalist, ask meaningful questions of the other person and listen twice as much as you talk. When you give your conversational partner your undivided attention to listening to their favourite topic i.e. themselves, they will think you are a good listener and are likely to be very open to you.

As answered on Quora.com.

∾

" Spectacular achievement is always preceded by spectacular preparation." — Robert H. Schuller

"Even though you may want to move forward in your life, you may have one foot on the brakes. In order to be free, we must learn how to let go. Release the hurt. Release the fear. Refuse to entertain your old pain. The energy it takes to hang onto the past is holding you back from a new life. What is it you would let go of today?" — Mary Manin Morrissey

"Desire is the starting point of all achievement, not a hope, not a wish, but a keen pulsating desire which transcends everything." — Napoleon Hill

31. QUESTION: IN WHAT WAY IS CAREER OR BUSINESS NETWORKING THE SAME AS MAKING GOOD FRIENDS?

A nswer Provided:
I'm going to take a contrary position and say it isn't, in my opinion.

Good friendships develop over time, based on many factors. Bill Doerr provided some excellent factors that foster development of a friendship i.e. trust, reciprocity, longevity, fragility and maintenance.

Where I take exception is the use of the term 'good' when it comes to describing friends.

In our web of connections, we have what can be called our Crisis Circle. These are the people we can really count on. You should have at least four people who will be supportive in the event of death, illness, divorce or bankruptcy. They can include family, friends, your doctor or lawyer.

Then there's your Buddy Circle. Friends you have fun with, the people who accept you for who you are. There should be at least three people in this circle.

Next, the third circle, is your Professional Circle. These are people who know you professionally, can provide reference letters and can speak about the quality of your work and character. You need at least 12 people in this category.

The Fourth Circle is your casual friends circle. These are people you share ideas with. You may work with them or know them through organizations or volunteer work. Some may become closer friends and eventually form part of the more inner and intimate circles.

For those of us who have been active on Linkedin, our network of connections would likely fit into the Professional Circle. And many of our Facebook connections would fit into the Fourth Circle of casual friends.

The point I want to make here is we go through life we connect with countless numbers of people we either maintain contact with or not.

When we network for career or business purposes, it shouldn't be a numbers game. Think quality over quantity. With the right nurturing of the developing relationships, in time, some of these new connections may develop into good friends.

I believe the term 'friends' has been watered down as of late with the terminology becoming ensconced in Facebook practice. Having hundreds or thousands of 'friends' in Facebook does not mean you are well loved or even known for that matter. Try asking some of your distant Facebook friends for a loan of money and see what happens.

When it comes to business and career networking, I think one would be well advised to consider the possibilities. We will develop strong relationships and some weak ones. Weak ones can be nurtured if there is the possibility of mutual advantage. Perhaps not.

Some will develop into good friends, most won't. Probably the best way to make new friends is to be one yourself.

As answered on Quora.com.

~

32. QUESTION: WHAT ARE SOME TIPS WHEN COLLECTING BUSINESS CARDS?

A nswer Provided:

First tip... don't collect business cards.

A collection of business cards takes up room and doesn't serve a purpose. Think quality over quantity.

A collection of business cards merely indicates at some point in time, you may or may not have spoken to someone who gave you their business card.

It doesn't necessarily mean you connected with them. If you haven't, I would suspect if you were to contact them a few months past your initial meeting, they may not even remember you.

Your business card is a tool. It is a way to introduce yourself to another individual with the expectation you will mutually decide if you share common interests that may be leveraged into opportunities.

If I collect a business card and I see there is a possibility of opportunity, I will reach out to the individual. Perhaps it may be sending them some info that may be of interest to them, or perhaps invite them out for coffee.

I will also send them an invitation to connect on Linkedin, explaining where and when we met, in my invitation. Some will accept the invitation, others may not.

If I believe there is value in the connection i.e. that we really did connect, I will add their contact info to my Outlook Contacts for future reference.

As answered on Quora.com.

~

33. QUESTION: HOW DO YOU BECOME CONFIDENT IF YOU ARE A VERY SHY PERSON?

Answer Provided:

You ask a short simple question requiring a complex answer to do it justice.

It's far too easy for people who don't experience being shy and quiet to say 'just stop doing it.'

Life doesn't work that way.

Being shy and quiet is merely a manifestation of having a deficit of social skills and a lack of self-confidence in the area of socializing.

If you experience severe anxiety over the thought of getting out there and socializing, it would be a different matter.

Being shy and quiet is a temporary state. You can change it.

The first step of course is being open to making changes in your life. Learning to socialize better does require socializing more.

It can be helpful to go to social events with a more outgoing person. They can introduce you to people and you might be able to emulate the skills they possess when it comes to socializing.

Think of improving your social skills as a series of incremental steps. Each step you take should be evaluated and adjusted as needed.

I would suggest creating your own plan for socialization. It could be something as simple as talking to a stranger at the bus stop or while in line at a store.

It could be in participating in a 1 to 1 conversation at a networking session when somebody asks you a question. It could work up to your initiating the conversation.

One cure for being quiet, is actually having something to say. It can be helpful to be up-to-date on what is happening in your community or even the larger picture of your country.

As well as speaking or talking about a topic you know about, it can be equally as valuable in being a good listener. Asking questions to a person who is telling you a story can make you a great conversation-alist in the eyes of the story-teller.

Assuming you are over the age of 18, I would be remiss if I didn't mention the value of joining a Toastmasters club in your community. As a member you will help develop your communication skills, which in turn develops your self-confidence. It can be a great way to overcome your quiet, shy ways. It has worked for me.

~

34. QUESTION: WHAT IS THE MOST DIFFICULT THING ABOUT NETWORKING?

Answer Provided:

There likely isn't a definitive answer to this question.

Each and everyone of us is different. While there are difficulties that many networkers face, it isn't universal.

One person may have no problem with walking up to a stranger and introducing themselves, another person may be crippled with fear of having to undertake the same task.

Some people seem to have the gift of the gab. Others are perpetually tongue-tied.

Some can handle their liquor, others can't.

As for me, I have researched the fundamentals of business networking and put them in practice, I still find it difficult to walk up to a group of strangers and insert myself into their conversation. I know *how t*o do it, but would prefer not to.

As answered on Quora.com.

~

35. QUESTION: HOW DO I OVERCOME SOCIAL ANXIETY?

Answer Provided:

Calling it 'social anxiety' is great for mental health clinicians. We've always known it as *shyness*.

Shyness is a learned behaviour. We are conditioned to be shy by our circumstances in life. We aren't born with it. Experiences that have been unpleasant to us have a way of repeating themselves when we least expect it. Odds are, when we respond with shyness in a social situation, we wouldn't recognize that our response is conditioned or a reflex related to the original incident. Our conscious mind won't give us access to that memory. Yet we respond almost in the exact same way as we originally did.

The big pharmaceutical companies would have us believe that shyness is an illness i.e. social phobia (social anxiety) and they just happen to have a high priced pill to cure you of your illness. You don't cure shyness. It isn't an illness. You can however reduce the impact that it has upon your life and the limitations that it creates for you.

You also can't generalize the symptoms of shyness. Situations that cause you distress may not bother me or someone else at all and vice versa.

I've been plagued with shyness throughout my life. Many people who know me would find that hard to believe and often consider me to be an outgoing person. I'm not. My default mode is to be shy. What makes the difference for me is that I have worked hard at overcoming my shyness, in those social situations that have caused me problems. I have learned strategies that have helped. Not all the time though. I still feel anxiety when I walk into a crowded room and don't recognize anyone.

I liken my social awkwardness, i.e. shyness, to the way I am with parallel parking my pickup truck. I have been driving for over forty years and had to be proficient with parallel parking to pass my driving test to get my license. In the following years, I probably haven't used that skill more than a few times. Stopping in traffic, while everyone is watching me and getting angry at me while I make what seems like a hundred-wheel turns, is quite anxiety-producing. I also have a short neck and continuously looking over my shoulder to see where I am backing up can be quite painful. I tend to back up by sound and feel. When I hear or feel a bump, I stop! Probably not a good way to be. I certainly wouldn't appreciate it if someone else did that to my vehicle.

My solution to parking in a spot that requires the advanced skill of parallel parking… is to drive around the block to locate a parking spot that I can drive directly into, parallel with the curb. Problem solved!

Avoidance of a social situation, like avoiding parallel parking, can solve the immediate problem i.e. reduce the anxiety but it is not an effective coping skill.

Shyness can affect people differently. In my 40-year professional career as a registered nurse working in psychiatry/mental health, I am confident in the social interactions that I encounter, while at work. Daily, I work with people that are displaying a range of emotions and interpersonal conflict is commonplace.

On the other hand, my business life is quite a bit different. I don't have a business degree. I am self-taught in skills and processes that are necessary to operate a business. I don't have a proven track record of successful businesses to bounce off. As you might expect these self-imposed limitations can be problematic for me.

On the other, other hand... I have learned to take the skills that have served me well in one area of my life and applied them to other areas. I think this is the root of how to overcome social anxiety. As you increase your self-confidence, your social anxiety *should* reduce. I say should, because everyone is different.

Self-confidence can be another of those blanket-terms i.e. one-size-fits-all. Self-confidence doesn't work that way. We can be very confident in skills that we have in one area and not at all with others. I believe that to reduce our shyness we have to use those skills that we are confident in and build upon them to increase our self-confidence, targeted at reducing our shyness. You don't do this by osmosis. You have to actively take steps toward increasing your self-confidence. This isn't always easy or comfortable. It is often said that your real growth begins once you are out of your comfort zone.

It seems a simple enough concept, right? We'll see! Self-confidence isn't a final destination, for lack of a better word. You don't achieve self-confidence and then maintain it for the rest of your life without continuous practice.

"There isn't a ruler, a yard stick or a measuring tape in the entire world long enough to compute the STRENGTH and capabilities inside you." --- Paul Meyer

Self-confidence or more precisely *gaining* self-confidence, is an active process. It is necessary to continually challenge yourself with achieving a series of achievable goals. They may be extremely small goals and seemingly inconsequential, or they may be major goals. The trick is to celebrate our successes, big and small, then move forward to even more challenging ones.

As a shy networker myself, often crippled with fear in social gatherings, I decided to do something about it. The result was my book, Power Networking for Shy People: Tips & Techniques for Moving from Shy to Sly!

http://powernetworkingforshypeople.ca

(**PNSP**) In it I outline a system for introverts and shy introverts to level the playing field when it comes to networking for business. The often dreaded meeting and talking to another person, face-to-face, is only a small part of the process. Yet it is likely the part that gives us the most stress.

As writing **PNSP** unfolded, I realized that providing practical strategies for what I coined *power networking* specifically targeted at shy networkers, as well as providing strategies to reduce the actual social anxiety was beyond the scope of one manual. Those specific techniques will be covered in my upcoming book Shy to Sly! (working title).

I'm not going to elaborate here on all of the steps required to increase your self-confidence and become a better networker. I have outlined a systematic approach in the book. Other contributors to answering this question have provided some good suggestions. The problem is that the suggestions can be overcoming to a shy networker. The old adage comes to mind "How do you eat an elephant?" The answer being "one bite at a time." If you are going to change your life-long behaviours you need to do it in a systematic approach to be successful in the long run.

I would be remiss in not suggesting that membership in a Toastmasters club would go a long way in reducing one's shyness. It's not an automatic process though. Toastmasters provides ample opportunity to practice the skills you require to build your self-confidence as well as practical interactions where you can practice your 1-1 communication skills. Working with a fellow club member as a mentor that demonstrates skills in socializing can go a long way in building your own expertise in socializing.

My research into the subject of shyness aka social anxiety, is that it is a condition that can be reduced and effect a subsequent increase in self-confidence, with a step-by-step strategic plan in place. It is well within the reach of most of us.

The downside to this is that I have also confirmed that if you are actually crippled by social anxiety, a self-directed strategic approach may be limited in its success. If you can afford it, a professional psychologist specializing in reducing fears such as social anxiety may be a better option. Support groups run by mental health professionals, assuming you can find one, would be another good option. Overcoming shyness isn't a quick process but the debilitating anxiety and fears can be crippling to some people. I vote for change! Good luck!

~

"THE DIFFERENCE BETWEEN THE IMPOSSIBLE AND THE POSSIBLE LIES IN a man's determination." — Tommy Lasorda

"YOU WILL BECOME AS SMALL AS YOUR CONTROLLING DESIRE, OR AS great as your dominant aspiration."— Mark Victor Hansen

36. QUESTION: WHAT'S THE BEST APPROACH TO NETWORK AS A JOB SEEKER?

A nswer Provided:
I wouldn't consider any of your suggestions as 'best' approaches to network as a job seeker, including your 'besides leveraging existing comments'.

Your suggestions are all passive in nature. As a job-seeker, you really do need to get out there and market yourself via business networking i.e. face to face, belly to belly as the saying goes.

You didn't expand upon what you mean by leveraging your existing contacts. There is a lot more involved in the activity of 'leveraging' contacts than one might consider.

It involves some work and brain power. What you really need to do is leverage your connections, connections. These are your 2nd & 3rd degree connections.

You may think that you don't know anyone who can help you with your job search.

But you know more people than you think, and there's a very good chance that at least a few of these people know someone who can give you career advice or point you to a job opening.

You'll never know if you don't ask!

Some Job Search Coaches will tell you that leveraging your network is the most effective strategy you can use to find your ideal job.

The first step is to create a network web of connections. A *Network Web* is a tool that helps you draw upon your personal network to find the ideal job that you are looking for.

Your ideal job may not be posted yet, in fact, it may not even be created yet.

Your Network Web can help put you in front of decision makers and key people that are in the position to hire you.

Step One is to make a list of your personal categories.

These are your interests and the organizations, formal and informal that you belong to.

These may include hobbies, family, church, professional organizations, sports teams, current and past employment.

Create a page for each of the above categories as well as any others that you can think of.

Step Two is to make a list of people you know in each category, start with a list of 10 names for each organization or interest category and then add 10 more if possible.

Then you would create a diagram with four circles. Each one larger than the previous one and wrapped around the others. There should be enough room to add the names of your connections.

First Circle: The crisis circle is closest to the center of the Web.

These are the people you can really count on.

You should have at least four people who will be supportive in the event of death, illness, divorce or bankruptcy. They can include family, friends, your doctor or lawyer.

The Second Circle: This is your buddy circle. Friends you have fun with, the people who accept you for who you are.

There should be at least three people in this circle.

The Third Circle: This is your professional circle. People who you know professionally, can provide reference letters and can speak about the quality of your work and character.

You need at least 12 people in this category.

The Fourth Circle: This is your casual friends circle. People you can share ideas with. You may work with them or know them through organizations or volunteer work.

Some may become closer friends and eventually form part of the more inner and intimate circles.

Create a list of people under the four circle's headings e.g. My Crisis Circle... My Buddies Circle...

Likely, many of your Linkedin connections will fit into your Third Circle, your professional circle.

The Network Web is a powerful tool. You'll be amazed at all the contacts you do have, and can identify the gaps in the network.

With your goal of finding suitable employment in mind you can ask:

• Who do I need to know?

• Who do I need to bring into my circle?

• And who do I know that can introduce them to me?

All the connections in the world won't help you find a job if no one knows about your situation.

Once you've drawn up your list, start making contact with the people in your network.

Let them know that you're looking for a job.

Be specific about what kind of work you're looking for and ask them if they have any information or know anyone in a relevant field.

Don't assume that certain people won't be able to help.

You may be surprised by who they know.

Almost everyone knows what it's like to be out of work or looking for a job.

They'll sympathize with your situation.

Unemployment can be isolating and stressful.

By connecting with others, you're sure to get some much-needed encouragement, fellowship, and moral support.

Reconnecting with the people in your network can be fun—even if you have an agenda. The more this feels like a chore the more tedious and anxiety-ridden the process will be.

Focus on building relationships. Networking is a give-and-take process that involves making connections, sharing information, and asking questions.

It's a way of relating to others, not a technique for getting a job or a favour.

As answered on Quora.com.

~

37. QUESTION: WHY IS NETWORKING IMPORTANT IN THE WORKPLACE?

Answer Provided:

Is it important? That depends! It may not be important to everybody.

If you are a 'go to work' and 'keep your nose to the grindstone' type of person, it may not be. There are many shy introverts that don't see the value of networking or possess the skills to do so.

Then there are many others who can benefit from networking in the workplace. It can be helpful to be connected to the 'grapevine.' Networking can provide unexpected opportunities.

My professional career is as a Registered Nurse. I work in a small facility and usually work with the same people most of the time. We have worked together for some 15 to 20 years.

I work mostly days on the weekends and nights during the weekdays. I have little exposure to others that work in my system. That doesn't cause me any problems as in my stage of my career, I have little to be gained by networking.

My business life is a completely different story. It is necessary that I network and continue to develop my connections. In the business world its not who you know, but who knows that you know!

My intention is to become the 'go-to-person' when it comes to business networking. It is an ongoing process.

John Jantsch, from Duct Tape Marketing is often quoted as saying "If you aren't networking ... you aren't working."

I'm fond of another quote, not sure of where it originated "Networking isn't something you do before work, or after work... it is work!"

～

"WITHOUT A SENSE OF URGENCY, DESIRE LOSES ITS VALUE." — **Jim Rohn**

"DON'T WAIT FOR SHIP TO COME IN, SWIM OUT TO IT." — ANONYMOUS

"YOU CAN ACCOMPLISH VIRTUALLY ANYTHING IF YOU WANT IT BADLY **enough and if you are willing to work long enough and hard enough.**" — Brian Tracy

"IT DOESN'T MATTER WHICH SIDE OF THE FENCE YOU GET OFF ON **sometimes. What matters most is getting off! You cannot make progress without making decisions.**" — Jim Rohn

38. QUESTION: HOW DOES ONE NETWORK EFFECTIVELY WITHOUT SEEMING OR SOUNDING LIKE YOU'RE BRAGGING?

~

A nswer Provided:

If you are bragging when you are networking, you aren't doing it right.

If you are not self-promoting when networking… you aren't doing it right either.

Bragging and self-promoting are not the same thing.

American Cowboy Poet Walt Whitman is quoted as saying 'if you done it, it ain't bragging!'

The main purpose of networking is to expand your sphere of connections with contacts that share mutual interests and can mutually help each other.

To be able to support and refer someone to another, you have to know what they have to offer. They in turn should know what you have to offer.

To be able to learn about common interests, you need to spend some time with another person. Likely there won't be enough time at a networking event, so you need to see about meeting them for a coffee chat.

Back to the effectiveness of networking. One suggestion is that you have your elevator pitch fine-tuned. You need a version to introduce yourself to a group and you need one that is more personal to introduce yourself to one person at a time.

You also need to become skilled at ferreting out those areas of common interest to move the conversation forward quicker.

As answered on Quora.com.

≈

"Each one of us has a fire in our heart for something. It's our goal in life to find it and to keep it lit." ---Mary Lou Retton [American Olympic Gymnast]

"Every time you are tempted to react in the same old way, ask if you want to be a prisoner of the past or a pioneer of the future." — Deepak Chopra, Deepak East-Indian- American M.D., New Age Author, Lecturer

"Friends are those rare people who ask how we are and then wait to hear the answer." — Ed Cunningham

39. QUESTION: HOW DO YOU BUILD STRONG RELATIONSHIPS WITH CONTACTS TO STRENGTHEN YOUR NETWORK?

Answer Provided:

Teddy Burriss offers some excellent tips on how to strengthen your network. I had to agitate my wee gray cells to come up with some suggestions that would add to the discussion.

One of the things that I have found when it comes to building and strengthening business relationships is to actively discover the common interests that you and the other person have.

Once you discover commonalities you can leverage it for mutual advantage. Note that I didn't say 'exploit' for your advantage.

I belong to a morning breakfast referral networking group i.e. iNetwork Kelowna. One of our beliefs is that people do business with people that they know and trust. Trust comes from getting to know each other, what the other's business is all about and who would make a good referral for them. We do this by going out for business coffee meetings and getting to know each other.

Spending time with and getting to know your connection is the secret to strengthening the relationship bond.

Mr. Burris talks about 'lead with give, not need." Dr. Ivan Misner

Founder of BNI (Business Networking International) takes a little different tact of 'givers gain!'

Both are variations on a theme. When you do something favourable for another person i.e. your connection, a principal called the Law of Reciprocity kicks in.

What happens is that subconsciously the other person feels the need to repay your generosity. They feel the tension until they act upon it. Once they have repaid the perceived debt, they in turn are more likely to want to do something else for you.

You are not really exploiting them in this case either. A general contractor colleague of mine says that he only does business belly to belly. This addresses the earlier statement of doing business with people you know and trust.

I WOULD BE REMISS IF I DIDN'T RECOMMEND A BOOK THAT I HAVE written on the subject of building your business network. **Power Networking for Shy People: Tips & Techniques for Moving from Shy to Sly!** outlines a strategy for effective networking whether you are shy or not.

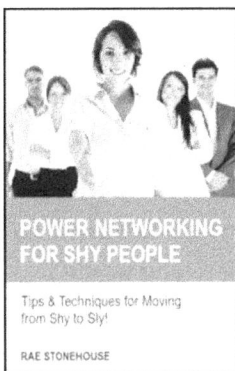

As answered on Quora.com.

40. QUESTION: CAN YOU DO TOO MUCH NETWORKING?

Answer Provided:
This question appears to be looking for a definitive answer, where only subjective responses will be provided.

If one defines 'networking' as the face-to-face or online interaction with another person, for business purposes and they spend all their time meeting people, at the expense of doing other activities involved in running a business, then perhaps you can do too much networking.

However, if you look at the process of networking as being composed of a series of activities, then perhaps not.

Effective networking is composed of the following activities [and likely even more!]:

· Face to face meeting and interaction

· Researching online the other person (before and after meeting them)

· Looking for areas of common interests

· Providing something of value to the other person (product/service) without expectation of something in return

· Keeping up to date with your connection's developments

· Providing public and personal recognition to your connections

· Connecting your connections with other connections for mutual benefits

· Providing referrals to connections that you trust

John Jantsch of Duct Tape Marketing is quoted as saying 'If you're not networking... you're not working!"

Networking needs to be part of your daily activities but not at the expense of running your business.

Thanks for your question.

As answered on Quora.com.

~

41. QUESTION: ARE MOST BUSINESS PROFESSIONALS GOOD AT NETWORKING?

A**nswer Provided:**

This question raises subjective responses.

From my perspective, of those business professionals that I know, I would say that they don't.

A comprehensive answer requires exploration of the terms 'good' and 'networking.' And 'business professionals' for that matter.

Business professionals isn't a one-size-fits-all category. There are introverts, extraverts, shy people and outgoing ones. The outgoing ones and the extraverts tend to enjoy networking more than the shy and introverted.

But just because a person is outgoing, that doesn't necessarily mean that they are 'good' at networking. Being a social butterfly or a chatterbox, doesn't necessarily mean that you are a good networker.

Effective *networking* requires strategy i.e. some thought behind what you are doing. It also involves having a purpose and a goal.

A COUPLE YEARS AGO, I WROTE A BOOK ENTITLED POWER NETWORKING

for Shy People: Tips & Techniques for Moving from Shy to Sly! It provides strategies for both shy and outgoing business networkers.

http://powernetworkingforshypeople.ca

As a business professional, networking is a tried and true method of not only increasing your connectedness but your earning potential.

I wasn't a good business networker. I'm not perfect yet but I'm a lot better than many and continually work on improving my effectiveness.

Thanks for your question!

As originally answered on Quora.com.

∽

42. QUESTION: WHAT ARE YOUR MOST EFFECTIVE CONVERSATION OPENERS IN NETWORKING SITUATIONS?

Answer Provided:

Effective? The risk is in not coming off like you're using a pick-up line.

I tend to use situational comments.

I'm not adverse to using "come here often?" It can elicit a chuckle or two and open the door to conversation.

Others:

"Is this your first time here?"

"Have you ever heard this fellow/woman speak before?"

"I don't think we've ever met. I'm Rae. Ray of sunshine!" also good for a laugh... sometimes.

"Gee, this weather sure sucks!"

I'm not so sure the conversational opener is the most important part. Perhaps the follow-up question to whatever their response is more important. You would want to go with an open-ended follow-up question to get them talking.

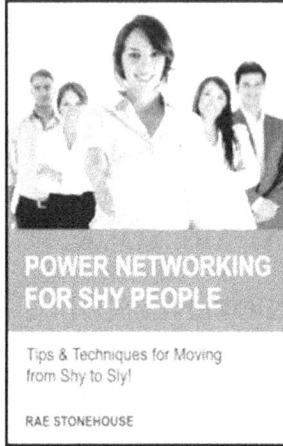

In my book *Power Networking for Shy People*: **Tips & Techniques for Moving from Shy to Sly!** I describe having a *Questions Toolbox*. The idea is that you prepare in advance for questions that can move a conversation forward. It also prepares you for questions that you don't want to answer.

http://powernetworkingforshypeople.ca

Most people like to talk about themselves and their business. And they can easily resonate with you if you are a good listener.

I enjoy a good conversation. Even though my default mode is a shy, introvert, I'm far more outgoing than most people. I find that if I take the lead in the conversation it usually goes well, as I have training in communications.

Thanks for your question.

As answered on Quora.com.

~

43. QUESTION: HOW DO I MEET LOCAL PEOPLE WITH COMMON INTERESTS?

Answer Provided:
A couple quick suggestions would be to check out Eventbrite & Meetup.

I don't know where you live of course, but both of these, offer access to special interest communities and may very well be local for you.

Another suggestion might be to see if you have any community recreation programs e.g. YMCA/YWCA, as they often have non-academic programs.

I would be remiss if I didn't mention Toastmasters International. Assuming you are over the age of 18, Toastmasters will likely provide everything you are looking for and more! Check out Toastmasters.org.

I have been a member for 23 years so far and it has changed my life for the better.

Thanks for your question and good luck in your personal journey!

As answered on Quora.com.

44. WHAT ARE GOOD NETWORKING EVENTS?

That really depends on what benchmarks you use to determine what is good or not.

I have heard of some business people that say if you get more than two free drink tickets with your admission, then it is a good networking event. Some use the food as a measuring stick, assuming there is any food served.

If you are actively looking for prospects, a networking event that provides lots of people to work through, i.e. by sheer numbers, a larger event is more likely to be beneficial to you.

If you are an outgoing person and confident in your schmoozing and networking, any size of networking event will probably work for you.

If you are actively looking to expand your connectivity, without regard to amassing prospects, any size of a networking event would work. Chambers of Commerce, business associations, entrepreneur societies, can all be a source of networking opportunities.

Another couple good sources of local networking opportunities are Meetup & Eventbrite. Just search for Business or Networking.

If you are a shy networker, smaller, more organized events may be more to your liking. I don't like the larger events. I don't like being hit on by the *sharks* who are out to make a quick sale, not into developing a relationship. I have better luck in connecting with smaller networking opportunities.

If you would like to learn more about networking, whether shy or not, I would recommend by book **Power Networking for Shy People: Tips & Techniques for Moving from Shy to Sly!**

http://powernetworkingforshypeople.ca

Thanks for your question!

As answered on Quora.com.

~

"NOW IS THE ONLY TIME THERE IS. MAKE YOUR NOW WOW, YOUR minutes miracles, and your days pay. Your life will have been magnificently lived and invested, and when you die you will have made a difference." — Mark Victor Hansen

"I HAVE HAD DREAMS AND I HAVE HAD NIGHTMARES, BUT I HAVE conquered my nightmares because of my dreams." — Dr. Jonas Salk

"THE PERSON WHO GOES FARTHEST IS GENERALLY THE ONE WHO IS willing to do and dare. The sure thing boat never gets far from shore." — Dale Carnegie

45. QUESTION: WHAT RESEARCH EXISTS ABOUT PROFESSIONAL NETWORKING GROUPS?

I'm trying to understand the entire market of "professional networking groups" including what are the largest groups, how many people attend, what professions utilize professional networking etc. Thanks in advance for your help.

Answer Provided:

From my experience, there is very little research, if any on the subject of professional networking groups. Just to clarify the question a little I would expect that you are asking about groups where professionals network, rather than networking groups that are professional in nature. Professional Associations, might meet that criteria.

A couple years ago I decided to research the topic of networking for business purposes. I found that there were a few books that were of value, but I didn't really find anything that offered sage advice i.e. from somebody that was speaking to me. My challenges with networking aren't generic, they are specific to me.

In a search of the internet I found literally hundreds of articles on the subject of business networking and since then I have collected hundreds more. In reading these articles a theme became apparent to me.

There is a saying in the comedy business, apparently only ever heard by me as nobody else has, that there are only seven original jokes in the world and that every joke is actually a version of these seven. We have our knock-knock jokes, which arguably aren't even jokes. We have the travelling salesman. We have two or three walking into a bar... that would hurt! We have puns, the lowest form of humour... unless it's your own!

I found this to be evident in reviewing the articles. There seem to be a limited number of themes based on the subject of business networking and each writer seemed to be basing their content on what they read in someone else's article. I wasn't seeing anything new or any original ideas.

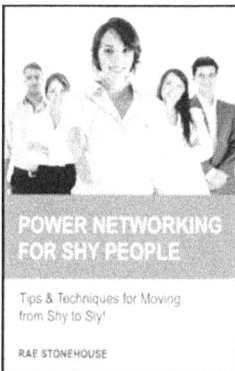

So I created my own book on business networking Power Networking for Shy People: Tips & Techniques for Moving from Shy to Sly!

http://powernetworkingforshypeople.ca

In it I provide sage advice i.e. practical advice that works. I outline a strategy that levels the networking playing field for introverts and extraverts. I have given a couple dozen workshops/seminars on the techniques that I have developed and have received favourable feedback.

If I was looking for specific research on the effectiveness of business networking I would check out BNI (Business Networking International). I believe they are the recognized leaders in referral networking groups. Their data may be more anecdotal in nature but I believe there would be value to it.

As answered on Quora.com.

~

46. QUESTION: WHAT IS THE BEST WAY TO NETWORK?

A nswer Provided:

I don't think that there is an absolute answer to this question. The answer probably lies in one's ability to take advantage of different networking models.

If you are a shy introvert, utilizing the internet in advance to learn more about the people you are going to be networking with, reducing your anxiety and building your self-confidence, then Linked in can be of use. I outline a system I created in my book *Power Networking for Shy People: Tips & Techniques for Moving from Shy to Sly!*

http://powernetworkingforshypeople.ca

There is on-line networking and face-to-face networking. While there are many venue types for networking e.g., Chamber of Commerce After Hours, Meetups, BNIs, breakfast networking groups etc., each has its advantages and disadvantages. In most cases they are good for lead generation as in setting up coffee chats with people to get to know them better and explore possible mutual benefits. They are not really designed for doing business or making the sale.

I think the best way to network is to develop a system that works for you, generates good connections/leads and provides a win-win scenario for whoever you are networking with.

Good luck in your networking! If you are on Linkedin, send me an invite to connect reminding me of our connection.

∼

KNOWING IS NOT ENOUGH; WE MUST APPLY. WILLING IS NOT ENOUGH WE must do. — Goethe

"DETERMINATION GIVES YOU THE RESOLVE TO KEEP GOING IN SPITE OF the roadblocks that lay before you."— Denis Waitley

"YOU'VE GOT TO GET UP EVERY MORNING WITH DETERMINATION IF you're going to go to bed with satisfaction." — George Lorimer

47. QUESTION: HOW DO YOU BECOME CONFIDENT IF YOU ARE A VERY SHY PERSON?

Answer Provided:

You ask a short simple question that requires a complex answer to do it justice.

It's far too easy for people that don't experience being shy and quiet to say 'just stop doing it.'

Life doesn't work that way.

Being shy and quiet is merely a manifestation of having a deficit of social skills and a lack of self-confidence in the area of socializing.

If you experience severe anxiety over the thought of getting out there and socializing, it would be a different matter.

Being shy and quiet is a temporary state. You can change it.

The first step of course is being open to making changes in your life. Learning to socialize better does require socializing more.

It can be helpful to go to social events with a more outgoing person. They can introduce you to people and you might be able to emulate the skills that they possess when it comes to socializing.

Think of improving your social skills as a series of incremental steps. Each step that you take should be evaluated and adjusted as needed.

I would suggest creating your own plan for socialization. It could be something as simple as talking to a stranger at the bus stop or while in line at a store.

It could be in participating in a 1 to 1 conversation at a networking session when somebody asks you a question. It could work up to your initiating the conversation.

One cure for being quiet, is actually having something to say. It can be helpful to be up-to-date on what is happening in your community or even the larger picture of your country.

As well as speaking or talking about a topic you know about, it can be equally as valuable in being a good listener. Asking questions to a person who is telling you a story can make you a great conversationalist in the eyes of the story-teller.

Assuming you are over the age of 18, I would be remiss if I didn't mention the value of joining a Toastmasters club in your community. As a member you will help develop your communication skills, which in turn develops your self-confidence. It can be a great way to overcome your quiet, shy ways. It has worked for me.

Originally answered on Quora.com.

~

48. QUESTION: WHAT ARE SOME SPEED NETWORKING TIPS?

Answer provided:

I'm not sure how to interpret this question. One way would be that the question is looking for tips from professional speed networkers. This would presume that there is a subsector of elite networkers that consider themselves professionals. If so, I would expect that they are self-proclaimed professionals. That leads me to wonder that if they are so good, why do they have to keep producing more connections? Wouldn't it be better to build quality relationships with the number of connections they already have i.e. quality over quantity?

Another perspective is that the question is asking for speed networking tips from business professionals that are successful using the format of speed networking. I'll go with the latter.

Speed networking is an organized event where the expectation is that all of the participants will have access to a greater number of personal interactions then they would on their own or at a typical, non-organized meet and greet.

This question is asking for tips i.e. what works and perhaps what doesn't. Here are some to consider based on my experience and opinion.

1. While meeting a large number of people and collecting an equal amount of business cards can look like a measure of success, when it comes to networking and developing relationships, quality is better than quantity. Despite their being a large number of people to meet, you may be more productive with deciding on a number in advance as to how many new people you want to meet. Perhaps 5 to 8 might be a workable number. I find that too high as I tend to forget who was who.

2. In a formalized speed networking event, where you are matched with somebody you already know, there may be advantage to finding more about them and re-establishing your existing relationship.

3. In a less formalized networking event, where you meet someone you already know, there is value in touching base with them. Some so-called networking experts will say that you should never talk to someone you already know as it is a waste of time and they aren't bringing you any new connections and subsequent sales. I totally disagree with that concept. I wouldn't spend a lot of time with a contact or friend but I would touch base to see what is new in their business or personal world and provide them with a brief glance into mine. I would also ask them if they know of anybody at the event that I really should meet and if they would be able to introduce me.

4. Be aware of whether the event that is being billed as a speed networking event actually is one. I am aware of some business association events that while they purport to be a business event, the members themselves view it as a meat market. No I don't mean 'meet.' Many of the participants are hoping to score at the event.

5. Don't spend too much time with any individual participant. Once the formalities are out of the way don't be afraid of being forward and saying something to the effect of "I think we may have something in common or perhaps we can be of

help to each other. Are you interested in going out for coffee to talk some more about it?"

6. Be ready with an exit plan should you meet up with someone who is dominating the conversation or you are receiving bad vibes from. It is a fact of life that we will not get along with everyone that we encounter. If you have a sense that something is not right, odds are that they aren't.

7. Be assertive when it comes to sharing information. "Show me yours and I'll show you mine" comes to mind. If the other person is dominating the conversation either be prepared to steer it in your direction or have an exit strategy.

I could fill pages on this topic and actually have. I expand upon these tips and many more in my book **Power Networking for Shy People: Tips & Techniques for Moving from Shy to Sly!.** The book isn't just for shy people, it is for anyone who wants to be more effective with networking measures.

http://powernetworkingforshypeople.ca

If you are interested in learning more about networking, visit my website at http://powernetworkingnow.com for my series of articles called "Is Your Net Working?

Or on **Facebook** https://www.facebook.com/PowerNetworkingNow/

Twitter https://twitter.com/powernetworkr

Youtube: https://www.youtube.com/user/ShytoSly

Linkedin: Power Networking Now https://www.linkedin.com/groups/4967132

As answered on Quora.com.

49. QUESTION: WHAT IS THE BEST SELF-INTRODUCTION?

A nswer Provided:

A ONE-SIZE-FITS-ALL RESPONSE DOESN'T WORK WITH THIS QUESTION.
The best self-introduction is the one that you are comfortable delivering and that serves your purpose.

In my article **How High Does Your Elevator Go?,** I suggest that you prepare several different versions of your elevator pitch i.e. self-introduction, as well as different time lengths.

How long should your elevator pitch be? Good question! Answer... It depends. Not much of an answer at first glance, but it really depends on the norms or the culture for location or venue of the networking session. Presenting your 30 minute curriculum vitae wouldn't likely go over very well in a round-robin style of group introduction where the expectation is 30 seconds, not 30 minutes.

Many referral networking breakfast/luncheon groups based on the BNI (Business Networking International) model, limit their members to 30 second elevator pitches. The more members, the longer the activity takes, but at least it gives everyone an opportunity to speak.

The problem is that many people get so used to delivering a 30 second infomercial about themselves that they can't adapt to being given a longer time allotment. Another problem that I see often is that many people create their elevator pitch around their business or what they do for a living. While that may be great for a business or workplace networking opportunity, not so in a social gathering or perhaps an event that has no connection to their career or profession.

I'm of the belief that you should have multiple versions of your self-introduction that you can pull out of your networking toolbox at a moment's notice.

Let's differentiate self-introductions based on large group settings vs one-to-one.

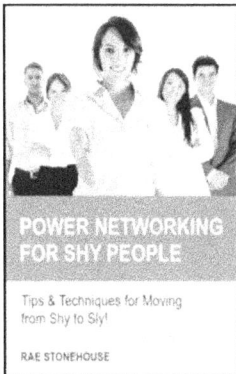

Here is a short excerpt from my book **Power Networking for Shy People: Tips & Techniques for Moving from Shy to Sly!** on the subject of personal branding and developing your unique elevator pitch. You want to be memorable. The advice provided is in relation to self-introducing to a large group.

http://powernetworkingforshypeople.ca

Power Networking Logistics:

1. Answer the question... "Who am I?"
2. Develop a personal brand. What do you want the public to know about you?

What do you stand for?

If you were asked to describe yourself in one word or perhaps a few, what would they be? If I were to ask a colleague or friend of yours the same question, would they offer the same words that you do?

Power Networking Logistics:

1. What words would you use to describe yourself?
2. Answer the question... "What do I stand for?"
3. Ask friends and colleagues in your existing network what words they would use to describe you.
4. Ask your friends and colleagues if they believe that you "walk your talk."
5. If they reply "No, you don't", what will you now do with this information?

Your USP:

Your **unique selling proposition** (a.k.a. **unique selling point**, universal selling point or **USP**) is a marketing concept used to differentiate yourself from your competitors or others in the market place.

Some good current examples of products with a clear USP are:

- Head & Shoulders: "You get rid of dandruff"

Some unique propositions that were pioneers when they were introduced:

- Domino's Pizza: "You get fresh, hot pizza delivered to your door in 30 minutes or less—or it's free."
- FedEx: "When your package absolutely, positively has to get there overnight"
- M&M's: "Melts in your mouth, not in your hand"
- Metropolitan Life: "Get Met, It Pays"

Your challenge is to develop a USP that on one hand is short and to the point, yet is clear enough that it captures the essence of your business and will stick in the mind of whoever you are sharing it with. Having it prepared in advance, believing in it and being able to recite it with a moment's notice will go a long way in reducing your anxiety and fear which are all part of shyness.

I would also suggest researching your competitors or others that are in a similar business that are not necessarily your competitors to see if they have chosen a similar USP as you have. I am aware of two business coaches that chose a USP that had only one word that was different. That one word totally changed the context of the USP but it really upset one of the coaches accusing the other of stealing her idea, even though they had been developed independent of each other.

Then there is the one-to-one self-introduction that is commonplace in any networking event. I have seen many people deliver their elevator pitch as described above. And I have done so myself many times. I've decided though, that it comes across as rather stilted.

I believe it is much better to develop yet another version of your elevator pitch, a more personal one. This would be used when you are meeting someone for the first time at a networking opportunity. It should be short and sweet and provide enough information for the other person to get curious and ask you questions. Once again, your introduction should be consistent with the event or situation that you are networking in. I like to conclude my intro with a quick question. That allows me to provide further info without sounding like I'm a walking, talking infomercial.

Examples:

At a Toastmasters function: "Hi there, I'm Rae Stonehouse. I'm a DTM (Distinguished Toastmaster) and a Past District Governor. I'm from **Flying Solo Toastmasters** in Kelowna, British Columbia. How about you?"

At a local business networking event: "Hi there, I'm Rae Stonehouse. My business is **Okanagan Help4Biz** and I provide solutions to problems that many small businesses face. How's your business going?"

At a different local business networking event: "Hi there, I'm Rae Stonehouse aka Mr. Emcee. I'm a professional cat juggler. Metaphorically speaking of course! As an event organizer I take the hundreds of ideas that are flying through the air when organizing an event and I make sense of them."

At yet another local networking event: "Hi there, I'm Rae Stonehouse and I'm an author, speaker and speech coach. Do you do any public speaking?"

In conclusion, I would suggest creating several versions of your self-introductions. Try them out. Practice saying them out load in advance so that you are comfortable saying your intro. If it works, use it again. If it is uncomfortable, try changing it a little. Go forth and introduce yourself...

～

"THE CONTENT OF YOUR THOUGHTS AND PERSONAL BELIEFS CAN BE proven by a single indicator - your current results." — James A. Ray

"OUR GREATEST FEAR IS NOT THAT WE ARE INADEQUATE, BUT THAT WE are powerful beyond measure. It is our light, not our darkness, that frightens us. We ask ourselves, 'Who am I to be brilliant, gorgeous, handsome, talented and fabulous?' Actually, who are you not to be? You are a child of God, your playing small does not serve the world. There is nothing enlightened about shrinking so that other people won't feel insecure around you. We were born to make manifest the glory of God within us. It is not just in some; it is in everyone. And, as we let our light shine, we consciously give other people permission to do the same. As we are liberated from our fear, our presence automatically liberates others." — Nelson Mandela, Inaugural Speech

50. QUESTION: WHICH TOOLS OR APPS DO YOU USE TO NETWORK EFFECTIVELY AT EVENTS?

Answer Provided:

I'm not a person who would put the words 'tools or apps' in the same sentence as "networking effectively."

Networking effectively is belly to belly, face to face. Forget the electronic gadgets.

Talk to people. Get to know them. Allow them to get to know you. Build relationships.

Use the gadgetry before an event to research people that it could be advantageous to meet at the event. Linkedin is good for that.

Follow-up with people you meet at an event via phone call or e-mail. Sending an invitation to connect via Linkedin can be helpful.

As originally answered on Quora.com.

≈

51. QUESTION: WHAT'S THE BEST WAY TO NETWORK AT 27 WHEN YOU DON'T KNOW MANY PEOPLE AND IT SEEMS LIKE MOST PEOPLE ALREADY HAVE A NETWORK?

Answer Provided:

27 or 67, it doesn't really matter, the same principals and strategies apply when it comes to networking.

You ask what the best way to network 'when you don't know many people.' You have identified the gist of the problem i.e. you don't know many people. The short and simplistic answer to would be to get to know more people.

Everybody has to start from somewhere. The purpose of networking is to expand your reach of connections. Its not just a matter of meeting someone and adding them to your list of people you know, it's a matter of connecting with them. Connecting takes place when you spend some time getting to know the other person, learning what their interests in life are and seeing if you have any common interests. Once you do that, the next step is likely to be of service to your connection. Doing so helps cement the connection.

So how do you get to meet these people? On-line, via social media is one way but the best way is face to face. Belly to belly as some of my business colleagues would say.

I would suggest looking for events in your community that interest you and would likely be attractive to individuals that you want to connect with. Check out http://meetup.com and http://eventbrite.com to see if there are any events in your area that you can attend.

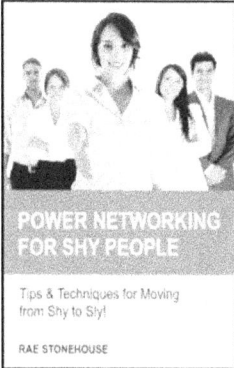

A few years ago I decided to do something about increasing my networking and increasing my connections. It resulted in me writing a book on the strategies that I created and tried out. I would recommend it to you. **Power Networking for Shy People: Tips & Techniques for Moving from Shy to Sly!** outlines strategies that will help you develop your network. It's available as a downloadable e-book.

Linkedin is a powerful tool for building your network. It is described in length in the book.

Good luck with your networking and building your connections.

As answered on Quora.com.

52. QUESTION: HOW DO I GET BETTER AT NETWORKING?

A nswer Provided:

A FEW YEARS AGO, I ASKED MYSELF THE VERY SAME QUESTION. THERE are some people that will tell you that they **absolutely** love networking. They will say something like "It's so much fun!" Yet, others, will tell you that they would rather have a *root canal* than attend a business networking event. As a shy introvert, networking was a painful activity for me. I've recently experienced a root canal and believe me... networking is much less painful.

John Jantsch from Duct Tape Marketing says that "networking isn't something that you do before work or after work... it is work!" You don't *need* to network to be in business but *you do* if you want to stay in business!

Networking is not a normal and easy activity for many people, especially if you are shy. It is a skill that must be learned and practiced. In business and in life, a majority of our success comes from talking to people and involving them in your ideas, plans, or projects.

Some people equate being an introvert to being shy. Not all shy people are introverts. Introversion is a description of where you draw your energy from. Introverts draw their energy from within. They often feel drained by being around people. It is an over-sensitivity to stimulation. Shyness is a fear and is a *learned* behaviour. It is a *conditioned* response. We weren't born with it. It can be a fear of the judgement of others or even the fear of judging yourself.

We can learn to change our behaviour. I know what it is like to be shy. I know how *avoidance* and *denial* can be a good friend. I know how *uncomfortable* it can be to attend a networking event and not know a *single person*.

I also got sick and tired of my inhibitions getting in the way of opportunity and decided to do something about it.

William Feathers, is often quoted as saying "knowledge is power." I'm not sure how Mr. Feathers was at networking but his statement wasn't true then and still isn't. Knowledge is only power when you do something with it.

In my book I share tips and techniques that I have learned to help you gain your power in networking and move you from *shy to sly*. If I can do it, you can do it too!

There is an old question that goes "How do you eat an elephant?" The profound yet simple answer is "one bite at a time." This Quora question and subsequent answers seems to provide a shotgun approach to becoming better at networking. I prefer a systems approach. With that in mind I will provide this article focussing on maximizing a networker's elevator pitch.

How High Does Your Elevator Go?

- 30 seconds? 60 seconds … 10 minutes?
- Different buildings?

Note: The following is an excerpt from **Power Networking for Shy People: Tips & Techniques for Moving from Shy to Sly!** By Rae Stonehouse.

The buzzword for conducting business effectively in the new millennium may very well prove to be "networking." In turn, the key element of a networking interaction is the *elevator pitch* or *elevator speech* as some would call it. We used them as children… "you show me yours and I'll show you mine!"

Well perhaps not quite the same but at its essence it's an opportunity to show your stuff and to learn about the other person. Assuming they follow the rules of course.

The basic premise is to imagine that you are sharing an elevator ride with a person who could be influential in advancing your business or career. You have the duration of the elevator ride to impress upon this individual why they should buy into your cause or at least agree to talk to you some more about it.

How long should my elevator pitch be? Good question! Answer… It depends. Not much of an answer at first glance, but it really depends on the norms or the culture for location or venue of the networking session. Presenting your 30-minute curriculum vitae wouldn't likely go over very well in a round-robin style of group introduction where the expectation is 30 seconds, not 30 minutes.

Many referral networking breakfast/luncheon groups based on the BNI (Business Networking International) model, limit their members to 30 second elevator pitches. The more members, the longer the activity takes, but at least it gives everyone an opportunity to speak.

Recently I organized a series of Power Networking Breakfasts. It was speed networking at its best, very much like a speed dating concept. Participants were allowed two minutes and thirty seconds to deliver their pitch. Time limits were rigidly followed with Toastmasters style speech timing lights, green, amber and red and a bell to signal the speaker to stop their pitch, then on to the next pitcher. The promotional material advised the participant to come prepared with a two-minute elevator pitch and to be prepared to answer a question or two about their pitch.

It was amazing to find that many of the participants faced challenges in trying to fill the two minutes. They had been programmed to speak and sit down within the restriction of 30 seconds. I believe that one of the challenges that many of us face is that we have been taught from an early age not to brag about ourselves. When it comes to business, if we don't promote ourselves or our business i.e. blow our own horn, then who will? We should be passionate about our businesses and be able to talk at length about what we do, why we do it and why you should do business with us. In fact, I would challenge you to be prepared to deliver a 30-minute presentation about yourself and/or your business. Arguably that would likely be one of the slowest elevator rides ever, but if you have ever found yourself stuck in one for an extended period of time, you will know that it could very well happen.

A challenge that I face is that with having multiple business ventures, volunteer roles, my professional career & pursuits, I could easily take the full thirty minutes for my 30 second pitch allotment. That doesn't leave any room for the others. If you find yourself in a similar situation I think that the answer lays in referring back to our analogy of the elevator ride. Many larger high rises have more than one elevator. I would challenge you to create multiple elevator pitches that you can use to match with the appropriate venue and situation. A social setting may be a good place to talk about some of the activities you are involved with and touching upon, but not going heavily into what you do for a living.

At a Toastmasters conference I would likely introduce myself as ...

"Good morning everyone, I'm Rae Stonehouse. I'm a Distinguished Toastmaster and have been a member for over twenty-four years. So far! I've served as our District 21 Governor a few years back and continue to serve our leaders in multiple roles. My passion is organizing and creating something from nothing. I'd love to hear how your Toastmasters experience has been. Rae Stonehouse." I've kept it short and sweet and hopefully have piqued someone's interest that they would want to talk to me some more. I haven't mentioned my profession or my business ventures at all. I will likely fit that into the follow-up conversation as the opportunity arises.

Here's an example of an elevator pitch that wouldn't be such a good idea. Let's say that I was in a meeting of the senior managers in my organization. It would probably not be well received if I were to give an introductory pitch highlighting my experience as a union activist. It would be much better to identify my name, my professional designation, where I work, how long and what I bring to the table.

I'm a firm believer in the adage "If the only tool you have in your toolbox is a hammer, than every problem will be a nail." I believe that to be an effective networker you need to have a selection of tools in your metaphorical toolbox. Having a selection of elevator pitches to be able to rely on for any situation is one such tool. Don't throw away that hammer though. Sometimes a hammer is exactly what is needed!

You can learn more power networking techniques in **Power Networking for Shy People: Tips & Techniques for Moving from Shy to Sly!** Available right now as a downloadable e-book.

http://powernetworkingforshypeople.ca

53. QUESTION: WHAT IS THE MOST DIFFICULT THING ABOUT NETWORKING?

Answer Provided:
There likely isn't a definitive answer to this question.

Each and everyone of us, is different. While there are difficulties that many networkers face, it isn't universal.

One person may have no problem with walking up to a stranger and introducing themselves, another person may be crippled with fear of having to undertake the same task.

Some people seem to have the gift of the gab. Others are perpetually tongue-tied.

Some can handle their liquor, others can't.

As for me, I have researched the fundamentals of business networking and put them in practice, I still find it difficult to walk up to a group of strangers and insert myself into their conversation. I know *how to* do it, but would prefer not to.

As originally answered on Quora.com.

∾

54. QUESTION: WHAT ADVICE CAN YOU GIVE TO SOMEONE WITH SOCIAL ANXIETY IN REGARDS TO JOB SEARCHING PROSPECTS?

Answer Provided:

Your question touches on two areas that I have personally experienced and have spent a great deal of time researching strategies to overcome.

In my e-book **Power Networking for Shy People: Tips & Techniques for Moving from Shy to Sly!** I outline strategies for shy networkers to level the playing field with those that are more outgoing.

Shyness and social anxiety are the same thing. We weren't born with it, we learned it. If we learned it, we can learn other techniques of overcoming or at least working within our anxiety and making it manageable.

A big part of how we experience social anxiety is what is called a 'self-fulfilling prophesy.'

We are expecting to be anxious, as we have in the past. So what happens? We become anxious because we always have in the past. We are talking about fear.

A commonly used acronym for FEAR is false expectations appearing real. That is the self-fulfilling prophesy in action.

When it comes to job searching and interviewing, it can often play havoc with our insecurities and increasing our social anxieties.

Many people believe that the employer holds all the power in a hiring situation and it is an unfair balance of power. This in turn increases our insecurities.

I believe that knowledge is power and that if you have it, you can increase your success rate.

That lead me to write and publish **You're Hired! Job Search Strategies That Work.**As the title says, I provide strategies to increase your personal power in the job searching process. The knowledge will help you gain the power to be effective in your job search.

Both increasing your knowledge of job searching and becoming more comfortable in social situations takes time.

When it comes to social anxiety specific to job searching it is likely related to the prospect of having to do cold calling i.e. to people you don't know, obtaining references and/or worrying about the idea of having to answer interview questions. At least that is how it was for me.

I would be remiss if I didn't mention that one of the best ways to reduce your social anxiety and in turn increase your self-confidence and the likelihood of landing a job, is to join Toastmasters.

As a 24-year member, I can't speak highly enough of the benefits and person growth that I have seen in myself and countless others. Check to see if there is a club in your community.

Question originally answered on Quora.com.

～

55. QUESTION: HOW DO I NETWORK WITH OTHER PEOPLE IN MY INDUSTRY?

Answer Provided:

I don't think anyone so far is actually answering your question. You are not enquiring about business networking events in general. You are asking about your industry, without providing what your industry is.

If I look at your situation strategically, I see several key areas for you to focus on.

Firstly, is the people you work with on a daily basis. Get to know them better. Find out how you can help them. Being of service to another without expectations of something in return can be one of the best ways to grow your network. This includes getting to know your supervisors and managers.

Secondly, expand your circle of contacts. Who are your customers, clients and people you deal with on a regular basis that aren't fellow employees?

Thirdly, is to think of a bigger picture. What industry do you work in? Do they have professional development or training opportunities?

This can put you in contact with people in the same industry, yet working for a different company.

Does your industry have an Association? Associations often have annual or more often meetings where you can attend and get a larger and more diverse group of potential contacts.

As originally answered on Quora.com.

~

"NETWORKING IS SIMPLY THE CULTIVATING OF MUTUALLY BENEFICIAL, give and take, win-win relationships. It works best, however, when emphasizing the 'give' part." — Bob Burg

"NETWORK CONTINUALLY -- 85 PERCENT OF ALL JOBS ARE FILLED through contacts and personal references." — Brian Tracy

56. QUESTION: WHAT ARE SOME OF THE BEST NETWORKING TIPS YOU'VE HEARD?

A nswer Provided:

Here is a tongue-in-cheek excerpt from my book **Power Networking for Shy People: Tips & Techniques for Moving from Shy to Sly!**

Top 15 Networking No- Nos

Throughout my publications I have provided tips & techniques to help improve your networking effectiveness. I thought it would be interesting and perhaps entertaining to take a look at the subject from a different perspective i.e. what you really shouldn't do.

These aren't provided in any order of priority. See if you recognize any of them from your adventures in networking land.

1. No Show: (Not showing up for an appointment) When all is said and done it can be argued that all you really own in life is your reputation. There are some people that don't respect other people's time. They make appointments that they don't intend to keep, or they pre-empt the appointment for something that is more important than meeting with you. Soon they get the reputation of not being reliable or keeping commitments. Is this the reputation that you want to develop?

2. No Follow-up: (Not following up on something that you said that you would do) BNI (Business Network International) founder Dr. Ivan Misner promotes the concept of "givers gain." Offering to help someone with something or providing information that can help an individual move their business forward without expecting compensation is a good way to develop a network connection. Not following-up on what you said you were going to do takes away from your credibility and your reputation.

3. No Follow-up: (Not following through with contacting a connection) If you say that you are going to follow-up with someone ... do so. If you don't at the least, you have missed an opportunity to develop a potential profitable connection. At the worst, well who knows! See previous article **Follow-up is Everything!** for an expanded version of why you should follow-up.

4. Not focusing on your conversation partner i.e. looking around the room for a better offer. I think that we are guilty of this at one time or another. Let's face it, not everybody is all that interesting to listen to. And you know what ... our conversation partner might be thinking the same thing about us! Listening is a skill. You will find that the more that you listen to people, the more that they think that you are interested in them, the more that they will reveal about themselves and they will think that you are a fantastic conversationalist.

5. Sexist or racist language. I hear this far too often in conversations with people that should know better. It isn't acceptable and I don't want to hear it.

6. Fly undone! Gents for heaven's sake check your fly when you leave the restroom. It might be a great conversation starter "So the bull's ready to get out is it?" But is this where you want the conversation to go? It can be challenging to recover from a position of embarrassment. Trust me I know. I was on stage for two hours once as an emcee with my fly undone :-(

7. I'm so wonderful! (Going on and on about yourself and not giving the other person a chance to talk) If you have been on the receiving end of listening to one of these types you will know that it is not fun. I would suggest hitting the Pause button and move on to the next opportunity.

8. Talking about someone else i.e. a third party who isn't part of the conversation in a derogatory manner. Some people are happiest when they are putting somebody else down. If you participate with someone like this, you are validating their behaviour and you will likely soon be labelled the same way. This is basically gossip.

9. Dump job: (Using your conversational partner as a sounding board without asking their permission to do so) We all have challenges in life, problems that are bothering us right now. It won't help your networking success rate if you become known as a whiner. That's what counsellors are for.

10. Monopolizing the Other Person's Time. This is a little different than what is outlined in #7 I'm so Wonderful! If you are shy or uncomfortable with networking it can be easy to stay with one person longer than you should. You are depriving both of you the opportunity to meet other people.

11. Disrespecting a Business Card: People tend to take their business card quite seriously. It is an extension of who they are. We aren't as serious about it as say the Japanese however, picking your teeth with someone's business card is a not a great way to make friends and influence people.

12. Hit & Run: (Acting like a Shark) Sharks are a type of networker that go to a business networking event with the intent of making a sale right there, right now. They don't care about you or your business. They are only interested in what they can get from you. Don't be one! And don't allow yourself to be attacked by one either!

13. Not having Your Own Business Cards: This portrays the image that you are not a serious networker. If you haven't even taken the time to develop and produce business cards to promote yourself, then why would I want to do business with you? I have heard it said "Oh I don't do business cards. I take the time to write their name down on a piece of paper with their contact information. It's more personal, and then I contact them with "hey remember me?" "Lame, lame, lame." That's all I can say about that comment.

14. Eating Food While Conversing: Many networking events offer food & beverage. Balancing a paper plate in one hand and a drink in the other can be challenging when reaching your hand out to shake another's. My personal belief is that if I am eating, I will stand to the side and chow down, then when finished I will resume networking. I have had to stand an awfully long time with a plate of food in my hand, while listening to another to avoid appearing rude. Be careful of spinach dips. Spinach stuck to your teeth can take your conversational partner's focus to different directions than what you intended.

15. Networking While Inebriated: You are your own liquor control board. If you can't handle your liquor without getting mouthy, don't drink! What you say and do may come back to haunt you.

As originally answered on Quora.com.

∾

57. QUESTION: HOW DO I GET BETTER AT NETWORKING IN CONFERENCES AND EVENTS?

Answer Provided:

At the risk of starting off by stating the obvious, to get better at networking at conferences and events you have to actually attend them.

And then it isn't a matter of attending any conference or event. There needs to be a purpose to attending. What is your goal? What do you hope to achieve?

In my book **Power Networking for Shy People: Tips & Techniques for Moving from Shy to Sly!** I outline a series of steps that a networker can take to be a more effective networker.

Strategies include researching the event on-line. Learn all you can about the organization and what they are all about. Who are the leaders or the people of influence? What type of people go to their events and could there be anyone that would be worth your while meeting?

It isn't a matter of going in for the sale. It is more important to build relationships. You won't build the relationship at the event. You need to follow-up after the event. Invite your new connection out for coffee. Get to know them!

While it is great to meet and listen to other people's stories, you have to be prepared to promote yourself. This is where your elevator pitch and your USP [Universal Sales Proposition] comes into play. What makes you different from everybody else?

You only improve your skills by practicing them. After a networking event, debrief yourself. What worked? What didn't? What will you do differently next time?

As originally answered on Quora.com.

～

"IT IS A MISTAKE TO SUPPOSE THAT MEN SUCCEED THROUGH SUCCESS; they much oftener succeed through failures. Precept, study, advice, and example could never have taught them so well as failure has done." — Samuel Smiles

"TAKE TIME TO GATHER UP THE PAST SO THAT YOU WILL BE ABLE TO draw from your experiences and invest them in the future." — Jim Rohn

"MISTAKES ARE PAINFUL WHEN THEY HAPPEN, BUT YEARS LATER A collection of mistakes is what is called experience." — Denis Waitley

"Life is a succession of lessons which must be lived to be understood." — Ralph Waldo Emerson

"YOU MUST LEARN FROM YOUR PAST MISTAKES, BUT NOT LEAN ON YOUR past successes." — Denis Waitley

SECTION FOUR: BONUS MATERIAL

Originally published by Rae Stonehouse under the heading Is Your Net Working?

58. TOO SHY TO NETWORK? POWER NETWORKING TIPS & TECHNIQUES

S ound familiar?

- "Do your hands start *sweating* and your legs *shake* with the thought of having to not only attend a business networking session but *actually talk to people?*"

- "Do you feel paralyzed by the fear of rejection when you are at a business networking event?

- "Would you rather have a root canal than attend a business networking event?

- "Would you rather send an e-mail to a business lead than meet them in person?"

Well if any of these apply... you may be shy!

"Get over it!" That's what our extroverted friends would say. "Just do what we do!"

Life isn't that simple. We aren't all extroverts and it would probably be a noisy world if we were. **Being shy isn't a personal defect.**

You aren't the only one out there, even if it feels like it sometimes. The world is full of shy people and that *doesn't* prevent you from being an *effective* networker and **reaping the benefits** that networking can bring to your business.

Shyness can be defined as a reticence and self-consciousness, not just in stressful social situations but over all.

Studies in shyness back in 1972 at Stanford University's Shyness Clinic indicated that 40% of Americans considered themselves to be shy. Nowadays, closer to 50% are likely to say that they are shy. You would think that with all of the advancements in modern sciences and the humanities that we would become more outgoing. Perhaps all those advances are what are causing us to become shyer.

It has been said that it started with ATMs and Walkmans. We are no longer obligated to stand in line at our financial institutions to do our banking. We can do it with a machine. The opportunity to talk to your neighbour while standing in line is lost as well as small talk with the teller. Grocery stores and many other ones now have self-check-outs. No need to interact with a check-out clerk anymore. Walkmans allowed us to walk and listen to our music, for our ears only, a great way to escape unwanted conversations. The Walkman developed into MP3 players and smart phones that while getting smaller in size have offered us more ways to escape the real world.

The traditional family is no longer traditional. The days where the father went to work, the mother stayed home and the children went to school, all to come home at the end of the day to share a meal and their adventures of the day only exists in reruns of Leave it to Beaver. Traditional meals were replaced by TV dinners, then microwaveable ones. Fast food has become even faster and arguably not even food anymore. The opportunity to develop one's communication and conversing skills around the family dinner table may be lost forever.

I believe that you can place the condition of shyness on a continuum. On one end you would have an individual who is painfully shy. The mere thought of having to go to a networking event and conversing with people could be enough to cause them to have a panic attack. Any situation where one feels that they are likely to die is to be avoided at all costs.

At the other end of continuum would be someone who experiences some mild apprehension about participating in networking events. They feel the apprehension but go ahead and do it anyways.

So how do we move upwards on the continuum to the point where we are less apprehensive about meeting and socializing with people, even to the point of enjoying it?

As a registered nurse working most of my career in mental health I realize that there will be some individuals that will only be able to move forward by taking an anti-anxiety medication such as lorazepam to reduce their anxiety. This is only recommended for those that have severe difficulty and only for short term. Despite what some physicians will say, these medications are only to be used for short durations. Coming off of the medication can be as stressful for the person as the situation that the medication was taken for in the first place.

I believe that the secret to becoming more social i.e. moving away from shy is a cognitive behavioural one combined with skill development. There are a few clinical modalities that might be of use. Some might say that it is not important to know why you are shy or what causes your symptoms. "Forget about it, move forward, do it anyways!" A *Reality Therapy* approach might be "You are shy because you choose to be. What are you going to do to change it and become more social?"

A *Solutions Focused* approach would likely say something like "Tell me what it would look like if you were no longer shy. What would you be doing? Who would you be talking to? What would you be saying to them? How would you be feeling?" They wouldn't be focusing on the past, only on how the future *could* be.

I'm a proponent of the Solutions Focused Method combined with education and experience.

There are many parallels with the fear of public speaking and shyness in social situations. Over the past 20 years I have been honing my public speaking skills by studying public speaking as a member of Toastmasters. Both within my club with fellow members and out in the public I regularly challenge myself by delivering presentations and speeches.

Darren Lacroix, the 2001 World Champion of Public Speaking describes the secret to becoming a better public speaker as being "Stage time, stage time, stage time." I believe that the secret to becoming less shy and more self-confident is similar. You need to face your fear of networking by getting out there and doing it, over and over again.

Within the Toastmasters program we develop our skills by continually moving forward in our educational program and raising the bar as they say in increasing the challenges that we face. The more that we speak in public, the more that we desensitize ourselves and reduce the power that anxiety has over us. The Toastmaster's program also offers constructive feedback as a way to maximize our self-development.

An overall plan to reduce shyness and increase self-confidence would be wise to include joining Toastmasters. Membership will provide you plenty of opportunities to both develop your communication and leadership skills but also plenty of opportunities to network in social situations.

Research the topic of business networking. You will find that while there is lots written about the subject, finding practical tips and techniques can be challenging to find.

Look for networking events in your community. Don't expect to be a power networker from the beginning. As they say you can't expect to run before you can walk. Learn what you can about the organization facilitating the event. What type of people attend the events? Is it purely social in nature or are people expecting to network for business opportunities?

If you are shy and it is important that you network, accompany a friend to the next business networking event, preferably someone who is a little more outgoing than you are. Ask them to introduce you to some people that they know that may be of benefit for you to meet.

As I said in the introduction, if almost 50% of people are saying that they are shy, then odds are there will be a high number of shy people at any event. You won't be alone!

$$\approx$$

"TAKE TIME TO GATHER UP THE PAST SO THAT YOU WILL BE ABLE TO draw from your experiences and invest them in the future." — Jim Rohn

EXPERIENCE IS NOT WHAT HAPPENS TO A MAN, IT IS WHAT A MAN DOES with what happens to him. — Aldous Huxley, 1894-1963, British Author

"LIFE IS NOT JUST THE PASSING OF TIME. LIFE IS THE COLLECTION OF experiences and their intensity." — Jim Rohn

59. YOU GET BACK WHAT YOU GIVE: POWER NETWORKING TIPS & TECHNIQUES

I recently noticed the often used saying "You Get Back What You Give" written in large letters on a roadside display board at a local church. Perhaps they are stating the obvious but then one's base personality of being an optimist or a pessimist might come into play. Do you see the world as one of opportunity or as one of danger and threats?

If you are a believer in the law of attraction you have likely also heard the sayings "you reap what you sew" or "what you think about comes about." Dr. Ivan Misner, Founder of BNI describes this as the "Givers Gain" principal. The law of reciprocity says that if you provide a service or favour for another they will likely feel obligated to return the favour. I have read somewhere that it creates a tension in the individual who has received a favour to the extent that they feel a discomfort until they have returned the favour and evened the score. This may be at a subconscious level and they wouldn't even be aware of why they are doing it.

The example above refers to the results that can occur for helping another individual. Sometimes, cause and effect aren't related in time. Meaning that you can't always see your results nor can they always be attributed to your actions. The law of attraction would have you believe that if you put out something good to the Universe it will respond by having something good return to you. The results that you obtain aren't always related to the good that you put out though. It could come back to you from a different, perhaps unexpected source.

So what does this have to do with business networking? When you provide assistance or a favour for another individual without the expectation of gain, the Universe will balance it out and you will receive something in return. Providing a business referral to someone in your network could result in multiple referrals back to you.

An easy way to start this in motion is to create and submit a testimonial for someone in your network and submit it to their Linkedin profile under the appropriate heading i.e. where you have worked with them or know of their work. Odds are that they will become motivated to submit one in return on your behalf. This action has an added benefit of displaying your name in their profile which is linked to yours. People are curious and frequently read the Linkedin testimonials. A well written one will reflect well on you.

Another easy favour that you can do for someone is to Like their Facebook page or a specific entry that they have made. It helps to give them credibility as well highlights your name somewhat. The same applies to Linkedin. Post a favourable comment on something an individual has written or click on the Like button.

We all have skills and expertise that we use everyday in our jobs and businesses. What we take for granted might be awe-inspiring in others. Consider doing some pro bono work for others. Doing so can significantly help someone in need and can also give you that warm fuzzy feeling that we sometimes crave. You never know what you will receive in return once you set this action in place.

If you know the person well enough and you are comfortable doing so, offer their name as a referral if someone is looking for a service or product that they provide.

Whether you believe in the law of attraction or not there is enough anecdotal evidence out there that indicates that the principal of "Givers Gain" actually works. I would challenge you to test it out and see for yourself. Try it and see what happens. Let me know how your net's working.

∾

"SOMEONE ONCE ASKED ME WHAT I WANT ON MY EPITAPH WHEN I PASS away. Just the words - 'I tried.' That's what this game of life is all about. Trying. There's the tryers, the criers, and the liars." — Mickey Rooney

"DO NOT LET WHAT YOU CANNOT DO INTERFERE WITH WHAT YOU CAN do." — John Wooden

"DESIRE IS THE KEY TO MOTIVATION, BUT IT'S THE DETERMINATION AND commitment to an unrelenting pursuit of your goal - a commitment to excellence - that will enable you to attain the success you seek."— Mario Andretti

"ALL GREAT MASTERS ARE CHIEFLY DISTINGUISHED BY THE POWER OF adding a second, a third, and perhaps a fourth step in a continuous line. Many a man had taken the first step. With every additional step you enhance immensely the value of your first." — Ralph Waldo Emerson

60. BE THE RED CAR: POWER NETWORKING TIPS & TECHNIQUES

At a recent networking event I made comment to a woman that since having met her within the past year I was starting to see her at a lot of different events. She replied "Yeah me to. You are the red car!"

I immediately recognized the red car reference from the Law of Attraction. The idea being that if you were to buy a red car or even were thinking about buying one, then you would start noticing red cars everywhere. The Universe recreates itself for you. Up until that point red cars were not in your range of focus.

Now when it comes to business networking it would be advantageous for you to become that red car i.e. someone that others recognize easily.

One way to become more visible would be to attend local events that provide networking opportunities and working the room so that you "touch" many people i.e. interact with them. If you attend an event regularly, people will get used to seeing you there. It could get to the point that if you aren't in attendance someone might say "I wonder where .... is?"

If you are not overly comfortable with interacting in a face-to-face situation, cyberspace can be a good resource for you. Social media venues such as Twitter, Facebook & Linkedin offer plenty of opportunities to create an on-line persona. By joining on-line groups that are locally based you can easily interact with business people that you might not meet at a networking event or in the normal course of operating your business. Both Linkedin and Facebook allow you to post updates which can help to keep your name front and centre. So when you actually do meet them in person you already have something in common to talk about.

I am very active on-line promoting my articles such as this one as well as my business and events that I am organizing. I also have quite a few websites that I have created and maintain. This tends to provide lots of entries in Google. If for whatever reason somebody was researching me, they would have lots of info to sift through. This works as a promotional tool for me.

I was at a Chamber of Commerce event and a young woman came up to me and said "I just had to meet you. You are everywhere!" She was referring to my presence on local social media venues. To her I had become the "red car." She was actively visiting local sites and my name and photo were popping up everywhere.

I believe that there is an accompanying assumption. If you are seen everywhere i.e. being the red car, you are obviously well-connected, that you have something of value to share and it would be worthwhile getting to know you.

How do you become the red car? It could be blue or any other colour if you don't care for red. If I had my way it would be a bright school bus-yellow pickup truck. But since I don't own one and it's on my wish list, perhaps seeing someone else driving one might not be so appreciated. I am a little leery about putting my thoughts about a new pickup truck out to the universe. The last time I did I had a new truck within a week. All I had to do was hit some black ice, do a 360 degree turnaround, land in a ditch, have the wheels fall off and have the truck written off.

So if you do become someone's "red truck" use your power wisely!

~

"A MEDIOCRE IDEA THAT GENERATES ENTHUSIASM WILL GO FURTHER than a great idea that inspires no one." —- Mary Kay Ash

"PEOPLE OFTEN SAY THAT MOTIVATION DOESN'T LAST. WELL, NEITHER does bathing that's why we recommend it daily." — Zig Ziglar

"THE MIND IS NOT A VESSEL TO BE FILLED, BUT A FIRE TO BE KINDLED." — Plutarch, Greek biographer, essayist (46-120 AD)

"A KEY CHARACTERISTIC OF TRANSFORMATIONAL LEADERS IS THAT THEY motivate people to do more than they originally expected to do." — Elizabeth Chell, British academic, management author (b.1949)

61. JOHNNY APPLESEED KNEW WHAT HE WAS DOING: POWER NETWORKING TIPS & TECHNIQUES

Legend has it that Johnny Appleseed traveled the American countryside spreading apple seeds randomly, everywhere he went.

In fact, according to Wikipedia, he planted nurseries rather than orchards, built fences around them to protect them from livestock, left the nurseries in the care of a neighbour who sold trees on shares, and returned every year or two to tend the nursery.

Many people's business networking activities can be a lot like randomly spreading those apple seeds. Some might grow but most likely left to their own, they will fail to develop and eventually die off.

Relationships need to be *nurtured*. Often the word *cultivated* is used to describe what needs to take place for a relationship to grow. Both words are really describing an active interest, desire and taking action oriented steps to develop a relationship with another individual.

So how does one *cultivate* a relationship? I have some cynical colleagues who would say that would treat them the same way as you would cultivate mushrooms. You keep them in the dark and feed them BS [male cow manure.] I would suspect that they have few quality connections. I certainly wouldn't want to be connected to them with that attitude.

Let's leave the agriculture analogy for a while and go to back to the question of how does one cultivate a relationship?

Consider these following steps or actions: (They aren't necessarily in the order that you would take. Relationship building can be more of a circuitous journey rather than a lineal one.)

- Research the individual. Check them out on Linkedin. Find out what their vocation and background is.
- Invite them out for coffee. Look for common interests.
- Be on the lookout for resource materials related to their interests and forward it on to them.
- Send them thank you notes or appropriate gifts to recognize help that they have provided to you.
- Send congratulatory messages e.g. cards/notes by snail mail or perhaps by e-mail for important milestones both personal and business. Seeing their name in the paper can be a great opportunity to drop them a note and congratulate them, assuming it wasn't in Crime Stoppers or the Most Wanted List of course.
- If you are comfortable in doing so, send them business referrals. The law of reciprocity says that if you do something good for somebody else they in turn will do something good for you.
- Perhaps you have heard of the concept of "unconditional love?" To successfully cultivate a relationship, you can't put terms in place. Doing so could jeopardize the relationship.
- Don't appear to be a stalker with your focused interest.

So far we have been looking at *active* steps that you can take. For a relationship to develop you have to be open to sharing of yourself. It can't be a one-way transaction. There has to be a payoff for you as well.

Getting back to that agricultural analogy of cultivating, sometimes you have to do some pruning to help strengthen your plantings. The same thing applies to your network. There will always be people that are suspicious of your motives or intentions. Perhaps this isn't somebody that you want in your network.

There will also be people that once you get to know them, you find that you really don't want to associate with them. It might be necessary to sever all ties with the individual. If you aren't comfortable dealing with or relating to an individual you are unlikely to want to refer them to another connection. Their behaviour could have the undesirable affect of reflecting on you and your business.

An interesting side note mentioned in the Wikipedia article stated that apple trees grown from seed are rarely sweet or tasty, more on the sour side, which was apparently perfect for producing hard cider and applejack back in those days. Modern day orchardists plant strains of trees that consistently produce a fruit that is desirable and marketable. There is no use in providing all the labour in cultivating a crop if you aren't able to realize a bountiful harvest.

So, when it comes to business networking will you randomly toss out those seeds or will you take your time and cultivate a manageable amount of productive connections? Your choice... sweet or sour?

≈

62. POWER NETWORKING SECRET REVEALED!

Okay, if you are thinking that is a pretty bold statement to make, I would agree with you.

Any time that you see the words "secret" and "revealed" together in the same sentence, I would advise caution. It is usually followed by a request for payment for the content of the secret to be revealed to you. I am going to reveal the secret to you for free, after all, it was given to me at no charge.

The secret to being a power networker is … [drum roll please] **ACTASIF**. Say what?

Simply put, to be a *power networker* i.e. one who is effective in their networking activities, ***act as if** you already are successful*. You may find it somewhat anticlimactic to hear this one word secret if you haven't heard the expression before. Another way of saying it would be "fake it until you make it." Or with a bit of a stretch it could be "mind over matter."

"Act as if it were impossible to fail." — Dorothea Brande

Apparently your mind doesn't know the difference between imagining and reality. You would think it would. I'm sure if I acted upon some of my imaginings as though they were real, I could find myself in a lot of trouble. So if your mind doesn't know the difference and you have the idea that you are going to be fearful or perhaps you expect the networking event to be extremely stressful, then guess what? It will be stressful and cause you to be afraid. On the other hand if you go to the event feeling confident, perhaps with the attitude of whatever happens … happens, then you might achieve different results.

> "The antidotes to fear and ignorance are desire and knowledge. Propel yourself forward by learning what you need to learn to do what you want to do." --- Brian Tracy

Any effective sports coach is using this technique extensively. They spend a lot of their time working with the athlete in having them envision every aspect of their performance in their minds long before the actual live event.

> "Never let the fear of striking out get in your way". – Babe Ruth, 1895-1948, American Baseball Player

If you are a Law of Attraction believer this is an example of a self-fulfilling prophecy, or even an example of the adage "You create your own reality."

My first experience with the **ACTASIF** philosophy was in my early years in Toastmasters. Toastmasters International is the world's leading provider of inexpensive communication & leadership skills training. As a new speaker I found it stressful to stand at the front of the room, with everybody staring at me and being acutely aware of my own nervousness. It surprised me to learn that even though I was shaking and fearful inside while delivering my presentation, it was not noticed by those watching and listening to me. There is a difference between inner & outer states. Yet, I am sure that we can all think of an example of a speaker that their outward appearance was one of terror, which would likely be a magnification of their interior state at the time.

What I learned was the power of imagery. Before my presentations I would stand at the front of the room or wherever my delivery area would be and I would envision myself being successful. In my mind I would see an audience that was hanging on every word that I said. They were nodding in appreciation of the content that I was delivering and they were laughing profusely at all of my jokes. I was a success ... even before I delivered the presentation. When it came time to deliver my presentation live, it wasn't stressful because I had already delivered the presentation in my mind and was successful. I will admit that quite often the live presentations didn't go quite as wonderful as in my imagination or some of the humour fell flat, but it didn't create any undue stress for me.

> "If you do not do the thing you fear, the fear controls your life." --- Brian Tracy

Every time that you make a presentation, and survive it, which you are likely to do so, you incrementally build your self-confidence. Self-confidence is somewhat like a bank account --- the more successes that you have in life the more that is added to your self-confidence balance.

When you undertake an endeavour that requires self-confidence, you dig into that balance and you use some of it. Unlike a bank account, using up some of your balance actually causes your balance to increase. The more risks that you take and successfully overcome, the more your self-confidence will increase. Unlike a bank account though, if you don't use it, you will lose it. Maintaining a healthy self-confidence level requires practice.

I have found this very same imagery technique i.e. ACTASIF to be successful when I attend networking events. Before going to the event, perhaps while I am driving there, I envision myself having good quality conversations with the people that I meet where I am not the least bit nervous. I see myself making some new connections that I can both provide value to and receive value in return.

I would challenge you to test this method. When preparing to attend a networking event that you usually would experience anxiety over try imagining yourself being successful with your networking. Envision yourself having successful and rewarding conversations. Then when you are actually at the event act as if you are successful. Don't forget, you already were successful in your mind. As Captain Jean Luc Picard from Star Trek Next Generation would say "Make it so!"

> "Most people are paralyzed by fear. Overcome it and you take charge of your life and your world." --- Mark Victor Hansen

63. SO WHAT'S YOUR STORY? POWER NETWORKING TIPS & TECHNIQUES

"Nice day eh?"

"To bad about the Canucks!"

"Isn't this weather something?"

We have heard them all before... meaningless comments that are more likely to end a conversation than to advance it.

For the many people that we encounter during our daily travels perhaps this is all that is needed. If we had long drawn out conversations with everyone, we likely wouldn't accomplish everything that we need to in a day.

However, attending and getting the most out of a business networking session is another story [pun intended]. This is the perfect opportunity for you to share your success stories. A success story is a short, punchy anecdote. It teaches your conversation partner about your business, what you are interested in and hopefully gives the listener a reason to get to know you better. All that in about 2 to 3 minutes!

This concept was reinforced to me recently when I attended a local Chamber of Commerce event. A fellow networker asked me how my society was going. At the time I was the Chairman for a local entrepreneur society. I went into my spiel of the challenges that we were facing in moving forward. One step forward, two steps backwards. I realized later that I had missed a perfect opportunity to promote the volunteer opportunities available within the society as well as the opportunity to share my vision for the future of the society. I have invested a lot of time and energy in moving the society forward and I should be prepared to share the story with whoever is willing to hear it.

It is often said that misery loves company. Does your present conversational companion really want to share your misery? I have met far too many people over the years that their default mode is what I call "poor pitiful me." I recognize it readily having used it myself in my early years. Many people find it easier to share with others how awful life is treating them rather than sharing success stories. The logical conclusion would be that if you were coming from a position of self-pity then you are unlikely to have a collection of success stories.

Many of our mothers have taught us not to talk about ourselves. "Nobody likes braggers!" Walt Whitman is quoted as saying "If you done it, it ain't bragging." While not grammatically correct, it is the essence of sharing your story.

Each of us has multiple personas based on the different roles that we have in life. Some describe it "as wearing many hats." We may be at a business networking session to market our business but we still have our different personas with us at all times and we should be prepared to share a success story related to any of those personas if the opportunity arises.

As in many endeavours, the key to success is advance preparation. Take stock of what is new and exciting in your life that others would appreciate hearing about. Share your enthusiasm!

So how does one create a good story? You would think that the answer would be to start at the beginning but you would be wrong. I would suggest that start creating your story by developing the ending first.

What do you hope to achieve by sharing a story? Are you hoping that someone will follow you in your cause? Will you be educating somebody on a topic or issue that is of importance to you or is your intention merely to entertain? The most important part to remember with developing your conclusion to your story is "What do you want the listener to take away from your story?"

With your "take away" clearly in your mind you can now carry on to developing your opening for your story. This is the part where you want to grab your listener's attention so that they are eager to listen to the rest of the story.

Using fishing with a rod as an analogy, your story's opening is the bait that you are using to attract the fish to bite. The content of your story being the moving the rod up and down praying for a bite. Setting the hook and landing the fish being the conclusion of your story.

I left out the part about drinking a lot of beer as I recall from my long ago days of fishing. Your story's opening should be short and to the point, yet be teasing enough for the listener to want to hear more.

A: "So what's new?"

B: "Not much, same ole, same ole. How about you?"

A: "The same. Business sucks. Can't make a decent living in this economy."

B: "We'll catch you later on the flip side."

A: "Okay, see ya."

Does this sound familiar? "A" set up the discussion with "So what's new?" "B" missed the opportunity to share a story about what is new and exciting in their life. Neither gained anything from this interaction.

You are at a business networking event and you are asked the very same question "So what's new?" Now what do you do? It's story time! If you have had previous conversations with this individual on a particular subject I would suggest updating them on anything new with the same subject.

If you haven't had previous conversation with your fellow networker, the field is wide open. You can talk about what's new and exciting about your business. Often there is an awkward period of time just after two networkers have introduced themselves to each other and delivered their elevator pitches. If they haven't found common areas of interest there can be a lull while each rapidly thinks of where to take the conversation. Instead of waiting for the "What's new" question, you could interject into the conversation and take it in a different direction. Yours!

So what's new? Go ahead ... ask me!

"I've been working as a registered nurse for over 35 years and having worked with thousands of people over the years I thought I had seen everything. The other day I ..."

"As a master organizer I help organizations create events that raise attention for their cause as well as much needed funds. One of my clients was pleasantly surprised when I..."

"Our entrepreneurs society helps create entrepreneurial leaders. We have a young woman working with us that has done some amazing things for us..."

"One of the things in life that I am passionate about is in honing my communication and leadership skills. I've been a member of Toastmasters for almost 20 years and continue to learn something new. The other day I learned..."

"I've been doing a lot of writing lately. One project is a series of articles related to business networking entitled "Is Your Net Working." My latest one is about..."

So... what's your story?

~

"WE DON'T WANT SATISFACTION. WE WANT CREATIVE DISSATISFACTION associated with excitement about the job. That's what motivation is made of." — Daniel Quinn Mills, US academic, management author (b.1941)

"DO YOU WANT TO SELL SUGAR WATER ALL YOUR LIFE, OR DO YOU WANT to come with me and change the world?" Steve Jobs, US executive, co-founder of Apple Inc (b.1955) persuading John Sculley to leave Pepsi Cola

"I'M SLOWLY BECOMING A CONVERT TO THE PRINCIPLE THAT YOU CAN'T motivate people to do things, you can only demotivate them. The primary job of the manager is not to empower but to remove obstacles." Scott Adams, US cartoonist, author (b.1957)

64. BECOME A THOUGHT LEADER: POWER NETWORKING TIPS & TECHNIQUES

W ikipedia defines a **thought leader** as being an individual or firm that is recognized as an authority in a specialized field and whose expertise is sought and often rewarded.

Would being recognized as a leader in your field or in your business make a difference to your bottom line? Is it possible for mere mortals, average people like you and I to become thought leaders?

I believe that it is not only possible to become a leader in your specific field but that it is in the reach of most of us to do so. With my keen interest in developing my business networking skills I am working towards becoming one of those thought leaders. I write about practical networking skills development for shy people as well as those that have some networking skills and want to improve their success rate.

Am I an expert at networking? In theory yes, in practice, not as much. I write about the subject of networking and shyness because they have caused me problems throughout my life. I've tested the tips & techniques that I offer and I know from first hand experience that they work. I also know that the lessons that I have learned can be very beneficial to others that are experiencing similar difficulties.

Recent studies have indicated that over 50% of Americans consider themselves to be shy. That is a huge market awaiting me to become an expert.

My researching the topic of networking has been educational for me in several ways. I have learned that I know more than a lot of people on the subject yet not as much as I could. My anxiety in networking situations has been steadily reducing as I become more educated on the subject and my effectiveness is increasing.

My goal is to become a thought leader on the subject of business networking. I am open to the fame and fortune that will come my way when I do so. It would be nice though if this happened a little sooner rather than later.

Is it really possible to become the thought leader on a subject that you are experienced with? Perhaps it might be helpful to replace the word "the" in the previous sentence with "a." You don't have to be *the* top expert on your subject. You can become one of many and still be an effective thought leader. You also don't have to compete on the world stage. Odds are that your local community and its surrounding geography could support you being its top thought leader on a specific subject.

So how does one become a thought leader? I will offer a few suggestions that you might want to consider.

To be a thought leader you actually have to give some thought to the subject that you want to be an expert in. That sounds rather obvious at first but I don't believe that it is. Many entrepreneurs and business people are caught up in working *in* their business rather than work-ing *on* their business. Day to day they provide a service or a product in their business without taking the time to think about how to grow their business so that they can realize even greater revenue. Becoming a thought leader involves investing in yourself.

I believe that it was Brian Tracy who said that if you read about a specific subject for one hour a day, in five years you will become a world leading expert on your subject. In essence, he is referring to becoming a thought leader. Thought leaders are well read.

Thought leaders are also well spoken. Many people believe that you are born with good public speaking skills or that it is a gift. There is no truth to that belief. Public speaking skills are no different than any other skills. You get better with practice and feedback providing corrective action. If you don't, you won't. It is also a matter of using it or losing it. To continually develop your public speaking skills you need to consistently work at it. I have been working on honing my communication skills over the past 20 years as a member of Toastmasters International, the world's leading inexpensive provider of communication and leadership skills development. Whether you are an experienced speaker looking for opportunities to speak or a beginning speaker wanting to get over your stage fright, Toastmasters is the place to do so.

Speak well, speak often!

Thought leaders are good writers. The old saying that "the pen is mightier than the sword" readily comes to mind. To be able to influence people and in turn lead them you need to be able to write in a manner that not only grabs the reader's attention it spurs them into taking action. The challenge is in writing so that your message is understood by the reader. The average North American reads at a grade seven level. Your challenge is to write so that they can understand it yet not have your material so dumbed down that you insult those with higher literacy skills.

On-line bulletin boards, chat rooms and social media venues such as Linkedin have helped level the playing field for those that tend to be on the shy side. You can be as bold as you want to be with your online persona.

Linkedin has a relatively new feature where you can follow Thought Leaders from around the world. Some of them like Sir Richard Branson have a couple million followers. I don't follow him but I guess a lot of people are interested in what he has to say. Others on the list have a mere 30000 followers. Wouldn't that be nice? It helps to look at that 30000 or so as being a number that could be achievable, assuming of course that it is something that you desired.

I'm guessing but I believe that Linkedin likely has a group dedicated to almost any subject that you can think of. You are allowed to follow and be a member of up to 50 groups at a time. To help gain exposure for yourself you can post questions or submit an article of interest to share with others. You can also provide answers or commentary on questions or discussions that others have posted. This can be a great way to create credibility for yourself and develop a reputation as being one who gives thought to a particular subject. It is also okay to disagree with what is written as long as you follow the rule of thumb of disagreeing with the opinion of the person rather than the person. There are ways to soften a response that differs from the writer such as "My experience has been a little different..."

To be a thought leader, or a leader of any type, you have to have followers. I am fond of a saying that goes "If you think that you are leading and you turn around and see that no one is following you, then you are really just out for a walk." I think that we all need to turn around every so often and see if anyone is following us.

We haven't answered the question yet of why we would even want to become a thought leader? Fame and fortune certainly would be nice but on a smaller scale there is great value in becoming the "go to" person if a problem arises that you have the expertise to resolve.

I have been lead to believe that the media is always looking for experts on a specific subject. It would be great to be on a short list of experts that the media reaches out to when they need a quote or sound byte on a topical subject. This is not only great attention for you but it also raises attention for your business. It can be a great conversation starter. Can you imagine being able to respond to the question of "so... what's new?" with "Oh, I was on the Oprah show last week." We might have to settle with an interview by the local AM radio station but you never know who is listening or what it might lead to.

Followers need leaders. If you lead, people will likely follow you. This can be an effective way to develop your business network. Get to know with your followers. Connect with them. Try it and see what happens. Let me know how your net's working.

∼

"IN EVERYONE'S LIFE, AT SOME TIME, OUR INNER FIRE GOES OUT. IT IS then burst into flames by an encounter with another human being. We should all be thankful for those people who rekindle the inner spirit." — Albert Schweitzer, Alsatian theologian (1875-1965)

US HUMORIST RONNIE SHAKES SAID: "I WAS GOING TO BUY A COPY OF The Power of Positive Thinking, and I thought: What the hell good would that do?"

WHEN ONE DOOR CLOSES; ANOTHER OPENS. BUT WE OFTEN LOOK SO regretfully upon the closed door that we don't see the one that has opened for us. — Alexander Graham Bell (1847-1922)

HE WHO REFUSES TO EMBRACE A UNIQUE OPPORTUNITY LOSES THE PRIZE as surely as if he had failed. — William James (1842-1910)

THE LINE BETWEEN FAILURE AND SUCCESS IS SO FINE THAT WE SCARCELY know when we pass it; so fine that we are often on the line and do not know it. — Elbert Hubbard (1856-1915)

65. FOR A GOOD TIME CALL ...

I am sure that most of us have heard of the practice of reading a message scrawled on a public restroom wall of "For a good time call..."

There is a usually a phone number accompanying the message. In all likelihood the individual mentioned is not aware of the advertising being done on their behalf nor would they likely agree with it. More than likely it was scrawled by an adolescent male, driven by testosterone and thinking it was pretty funny. Having not spent any time in the women's restroom I can only assume that this practice only happens in the men's.

If the individual named actually wrote the message in question well I guess it could be attributed to some savvy targeted marketing.

I am not suggesting that you add this to your networking skills repertoire. In my example the call for action is *"for a good time call..."* Each and everyone of us has something that we are offering, whether it be a skill or our expertise. When we are networking for business we need to get the message out there as to what we do and what we have to offer.

Now , using a plumber as an example, what if we changed the

message to something like for "For No More Leaky Pipes call..." A financial planner might say "We are your financial health experts. Will your money live as long as you do?" An entertainer could get away with "for a good time call..."

This in essence is your USP, which is often defined as Universal Sale Pitch or Unique Selling Proposition. Your USP is a short statement that summarizes who you are, what you do, why you are passionate about it and how you are different or better than anyone else who does it. All this in a short sentence. Yes it is definitely challenging. You may not want to do it but your competition likely is.

A memorable USP has a way of connecting you, your business and what you have to offer in a person's mind. You want your potential customer to automatically think of you when they have a problem to solve and that you are likely the solution to it. The only way that will happen is that you have to get in the habit of using your USP regularly, perhaps as part of your elevator pitch. You have to become known by your USP.

At the risk of self-promoting, after all I am an entrepreneur, I would offer one of my USPs. "Hi, I'm Rae Stonehouse also known as Mr. Emcee. I am on Okanagan-based full service master of ceremonies and event planner. From start to finish... we do it all!"

Or... for a good time call Rae... just not too early in the morning, too late in the evening, on weekends or in the afternoon as it cuts into my nap. But other than that...

～

66. HOW HIGH DOES YOUR ELEVATOR GO?

- 30 seconds? 60 seconds ... 10 minutes?
- Different buildings?

Note: The following is an excerpt from **Power Networking for Shy People: Tips & Techniques for Moving from Shy to Sly!** By Rae Stonehouse.

The buzzword for conducting business effectively in the new millennium may very well prove to be "networking." In turn, the key element of a networking interaction is the *elevator pitch* or *elevator speech* as some would call it. We used them as children... "you show me yours and I'll show you mine!"

Well perhaps not quite the same but at its essence it's an opportunity to show your stuff and to learn about the other person. Assuming they follow the rules of course.

The basic premise is to imagine that you are sharing an elevator ride with a person who could be influential in advancing your business or career. You have the duration of the elevator ride to impress upon this individual why they should buy into your cause or at least agree to talk to you some more about it.

How long should my elevator pitch be? Good question! Answer... It depends. Not much of an answer at first glance, but it really depends on the norms or the culture for location or venue of the networking session. Presenting your 30 minute curriculum vitae wouldn't likely go over very well in a round-robin style of group introduction where the expectation is 30 seconds, not 30 minutes.

Many referral networking breakfast/luncheon groups based on the BNI (Business Networking International) model, limit their members to 30 second elevator pitches. The more members, the longer the activity takes, but at least it gives everyone an opportunity to speak.

Recently I organized a series of Power Networking Breakfasts. It was speed networking at its best, very much like a speed dating concept. Participants were allowed two minutes and thirty seconds to deliver their pitch. Time limits were rigidly followed with Toastmasters style speech timing lights, green, amber and red and a bell to signal the speaker to stop their pitch, then on to the next pitcher. The promotional material advised the participant to come prepared with a two minute elevator pitch and to be prepared to answer a question or two about their pitch.

It was amazing to find that many of the participants faced challenges in trying to fill the two minutes. They had been programmed to speak and sit down within the restriction of 30 seconds. I believe that one of the challenges that many of us face is that we have been taught from an early age not to brag about ourselves. When it comes to business, if we don't promote ourselves or our business i.e. blow our own horn, then who will? We should be passionate about our businesses and be able to talk at length about what we do, why we do it and why you should do business with us. In fact, I would challenge you to be prepared to deliver a 30 minute presentation about yourself and/or your business. Arguably that would likely be one of the slowest elevator rides ever, but if you have ever found yourself stuck in one for an extended period of time, you will know that it could very well happen.

A challenge that I face is that with having multiple business ventures, volunteer roles, my professional career & pursuits, I could easily take the full thirty minutes for my 30 second pitch allotment. That doesn't leave any room for the others. If you find yourself in a similar situation I think that the answer lays in referring back to our analogy of the elevator ride. Many larger high rises have more than one elevator. I would challenge you to create multiple elevator pitches that you can use to match with the appropriate venue and situation. A social setting may be a good place to talk about some of the activities you are involved with and touching upon, but not going heavily into what you do for a living.

At a Toastmasters conference I would likely introduce myself as...

"Good morning everyone, I'm Rae Stonehouse. I'm a Distinguished Toastmaster and have been a member for over nineteen years. So far! I've served as our District 21 Governor a few years back and continue to serve our leaders in multiple roles. My passion is organizing and creating something from nothing. I'd love to hear how your Toastmasters experience has been. Rae Stonehouse." I've kept it short and sweet and hopefully have piqued someone's interest that they would want to talk to me some more. I haven't mentioned my profession or my business ventures at all. I will likely fit that into the follow-up conversation as the opportunity arises.

Here's an example of an elevator pitch that wouldn't be such a good idea. Let's say that I was in a meeting of the senior managers in my organization. It would probably not be well received if I were to give an introductory pitch highlighting my experience as a union activist. It would be much better to identify my name, my professional designation, where I work, how long and what I bring to the table.

I'm a firm believer in the adage "If the only tool you have in your toolbox is a hammer, than every problem will be a nail." I believe that to be an effective networker you need to have a selection of tools in your metaphorical toolbox. Having a selection of elevator pitches to be able to rely on for any situation is one such tool. Don't throw away that hammer though. Sometimes a hammer is exactly what is needed!

You can learn more power networking techniques in **Power Networking for Shy People: Tips & Techniques for Moving from Shy to Sly!** Available right now as a downloadable e-book.

http://powernetworkingforshypeople.ca

∼

ENTHUSIASM IS THE GREAT HILL-CLIMBER. — ELBERT HUBBARD (1856-1915)

HOW MANY A MAN HAS THROWN UP HIS HANDS AT A TIME WHEN A little more effort, a little more patience would have achieved success? — Elbert Hubbard (1856-1915)

THE FOLLIES A MAN REGRETS MOST IN HIS LIFE ARE THOSE WHICH HE didn't commit when he had the opportunity. — Helen Rowland (1876-1950)

AIM HIGH! IT IS NO HARDER ON YOUR GUN TO SHOOT THE FEATHERS OFF an eagle than to shoot the fur off a skunk. — Troy Moore

WELL DONE IS BETTER THAN WELL SAID. — BENJAMIN FRANKLIN (1706-1790)

67. SERENDIPITY ISN'T A PLAN! POWER NETWORKING TIPS & TECHNIQUES

I've often heard it said in reference to "self-help" books... "If you get only one gem or a useful tip from a book it makes all of your reading time worthwhile." While that may be true, it can have you spending a lot of time with your nose in a book.

The same principal can be applied... inefficiently... to your networking activities... "One contact can make a world of difference in your business ..." In essence you are leaving your success to serendipity.

Serendipity, or leaving everything to chance, while awe-inspiring when it works, is not something that you can control or count on.

Does the following scenario sound familiar? You attend a large event touted as the best networking event in town. You meet a dozen or so "new" people, new to you that is, not new to everyone else, or so it would seem. You deliver your 30 second or longer elevator pitch over the ever-increasing din in the packed room. You go home with a handful of business cards. The next day or so you face the challenge of contacting all of your warm leads. If this is an activity that you aren't fond of, that 200 pound phone handset can be quite daunting. "Hi, this is Rae. We met the other night at..." "Who?"

Okay, perhaps I am injecting my own inadequacies into this article but I really have heard people agree.

Here is a power networking technique to maximize your effectiveness. If your main purpose in attending a networking event is to get that handful of business cards, then go for it! An alternative option would be meet a business colleague or friend that you are comfortable with, in a setting that is conducive to conducting business and compare personal networks. "I'll show you mine... if you show me your's", so to speak. For those that are old enough to recall trading baseball or hockey player cards, this isn't what I am suggesting.

A planned approach is best. For example, I am looking for a bookkeeper/accountant to take on a volunteer role in a society that I lead. I would meet with somebody that I know has a background in finances and I could specifically ask them who they would know in their network that might meet my search parameters. At this preliminary stage it is a matter of brainstorming contact's names. Write them down on a piece of paper. This isn't the time to be evaluating each name as to whether they might be interested in participating, your only task at this point is to generate a list of names.

The idea is to leverage your colleague's network. With social media being so prevalent nowadays, many of us are well connected. Well-connected doesn't mean that we actually know or have even met the contact though. More of an e-contact if you will. It probably wouldn't be much of a surprise to find that you already know some of the names generated and they are part of your network.

Our next step is to rate each of the names that we have generated as to how well your colleague knows the individual. Would the individual be surprised if you contacted them saying that they were referred by your colleague? Or would your contacting the individual trigger a "Who?" response.

Generating a list of names isn't of much use unless you get their accompanying contact info. Now is the time to leverage your connections and make that net work. Make those phone calls.

PS: Don't forget to spend some time helping your colleague with their networking measures. While it can be said "It's not who you know... it's who knows you!", perhaps we need to amend it to "It's not who you know, it's who knows you know who you know!"

~

THE PRESENT TIME HAS ONE ADVANTAGE OVER EVERY OTHER - IT IS OUR own. — Charles Caleb Colton (1780-1832)

IS NOT THIS THE TRUE ROMANTIC FEELING--NOT TO DESIRE TO ESCAPE life; but to prevent life from escaping you? — Thomas Wolfe (1900-1938)

KEEP YOUR FACE TO THE SUNSHINE AND YOU CANNOT SEE THE SHADOW. — Helen Keller (1880-1968)

CHIEFLY THE MOULD OF A MAN'S FORTUNE IS IN HIS OWN HANDS. — SIR Francis Bacon (1561- 1626)

68. OVERCOMING SHYNESS IN NETWORKING: A SYSTEMATIC APPROACH

The following is an excerpt from Power Networking for Shy People: Tips & Techniques for Moving from Shy to Sly! written by Rae Stonehouse aka the "Shy Guy."

http://powernetworkingforshypeople.ca

～

AS THIS IS A BOOK ON NETWORKING FOR SHY PEOPLE, I'M ASSUMING that you experience shyness to a certain degree. There isn't a standard measurement that applies to everyone. We all experience it in a different way. What might intimidate me may not cause any distress to you at all.

For some people it is the large groups of people that cause their anxiety. For others, it can be the inevitable 1 to 1 conversation, where they fear that they may appear to be stupid.

For me, I find the approaching of somebody that I don't know to be challenging. I would suspect that I have a deep-seated fear of rejection that triggers my anxiety. Yet, I have developed an advanced skill at public speaking, an area that many would find to be even more stressful.

Darren Lacroix, a former Toastmasters International World Champion of Public Speaking Winner says that one of the secrets to becoming an effective public speaker is "stage time, stage time, stage time." Translation: you just have to do it over and over again.

I believe that the same principal applies to becoming a better networker. The more that you network, the more likely that you will become more comfortable with doing so. There is an expression that says "practice makes perfect." It isn't true! If you keep making the same mistakes over and over again, you just become better at making mistakes. Conversely, practice with constructive feedback can lead towards perfection. The Toastmasters International Communications Program is based on that very principal. I have been a member for over 21 years at the time of writing this and I experienced first-hand the benefits of constructive feedback. When you are networking there isn't somebody watching you so you will have to evaluate yourself as to how you did. This can be challenging as we tend to be self-critical especially in areas that we experience anxiety.

Networking Skills Self-Assessment

I would suggest developing some benchmark performance standards so that you can compare each new meeting or interaction. You would conduct this exercise later on after the event was finished. Some answers lead to yes or no answers. Others may be better answered on a sliding scale. If you keep records of your results you are better able to track your progress.

Some examples might be:

- I approached someone that I didn't know and made the first comment. Yes No
- I listened intently while the other person delivered their elevator pitch before starting mine.

- I was able to deliver my elevator speech comfortably.
- I was able to maintain eye contact for much of our discussion.
- I initiated an invitation to go out at a later date for coffee.
- I was comfortable/nervous in presenting my business card.
- I was comfortable in ending the conversation and moving on to another.
- I was able to ask some questions that moved the conversation forward.
- Overall I felt less or more nervous in comparison to other networking events.
- What did I learn about myself in this networking situation?

∾

USING DEVELOPING BETTER PUBLIC SPEAKING SKILLS AS AN EXAMPLE, WE find that new speakers tend to focus on what they see as their shortcomings. Their shortcomings take on a life of their own and minimize the skills and talents that the speaker already has. Research has shown that it is more effective to focus on the skills that you already have and strengthen them rather than focus on your own self-defined deficiencies. I believe that the same thing applies to networking and conducting 1 to 1 conversations. Find out where your skills are and use them more.

Use the benchmark assessment after each event and reward yourself for areas that you have shown improvement, especially those ones that have caused you considerable anxiety in the past.

So, what if I do the assessment and I am still having a lot of anxiety? I am really nervous around people.

As I mentioned earlier, shyness can be present in different degrees. Social anxiety can be a problem. I believe that managing social situations is a skill that needs to be developed. Like shyness or social anxiety, we are not likely born with well-developed social skills.

Your challenge is to reduce your anxiety to a manageable level. Having worked in the mental health field for over 30 years, often as nurse therapist, I'm not going to make a blanket statement to the effect of "get over it." There can be many causes of anxiety.

While I don't believe in Big Pharma's creating diagnoses such as "social anxiety" as a new market to sell their medications as a treatment, I do believe that if your anxiety appears to be excessive, you really should have a talk with your doctor. There may be other reasons for your anxiety that your doctor could help you with. Perhaps a mild antianxiety agent taken before you attend a networking session may help.

If your anxiety is excessive there may be an advantage to you if you were to seek out some help from someone with a psychological background i.e. a psychologist. Sometimes we can use a little help in getting past some obstacles that we have in life.

I had considered doing so at one point in my life to help me with interpersonal relationships but I chose a self-directed educational program instead. I found that one of my challenges was that I hadn't developed many of the interpersonal skills at an early age. As an adult I had to go back and learn the basics. My research exposed me to assertiveness training and communications, conflict and crisis management and systems thinking. As I mentioned earlier about having a tool box, the more skills & techniques that you have in your repertoire the less likely you are to become overwhelmed in a situation. If I had to make a single recommendation to anyone as to the secret of leading a successful life I would have to recommend the different areas that I researched. It certainly made my life easier.

Another technique that I have used in developing my public speaking skills is that of using imagery. Before delivering a presentation to a group or a venue that I'm not used to, I will go up to the front of the room i.e. where I will be delivering the speech from and I will imagine that I am speaking. I will imagine where everyone is seated. I will see their smiling faces and appreciation as to what I am saying. I see myself as being successful. So when I actually deliver my speech, I have already been successful in my mind. This helps reduce the anxiety that I might otherwise experience and allows me to focus on my delivery. The audience quite often doesn't react the same way in reality as they do in my imagination though. Five encores can be a little tiresome!

I believe that the same technique can be used prior to participating in a networking event. Imagine yourself being successful, talking to different people and feeling confident. There is a law of attraction principal that addresses creating your own reality. So conversely, if you go to the event with the expectation that you are going to have a stressful time, well then, guess what will happen?

Power Networking Logistics:

1. Practice announcing your name out loud.
2. Practice introducing someone else and deliver your introduction out loud.
3. Practice asking questions to another person while you are sharing elevator pitches.
4. During a 1 to 1 conversation with someone, invite them out to coffee.
5. Follow-up with them to set a date & time for the coffee meeting.
6. Ask some colleagues for feedback as to your attire that you are wearing to business networking functions. Is it appropriate and/or how could it be improved?
7. If you don't have a business card, have some printed.
8. Practice presenting and receiving business cards.
9. Purchase and start wearing a nametag to business networking events.
10. Practice your handshake at home and put it into practice at business networking events.
11. Practice maintaining eye contact in 1 to 1 discussions.
12. Complete the Networking Skills Self-Assessment.

69. FOLLOW-UP IS EVERYTHING! POWER NETWORKING TIPS & TECHNIQUES

I t can be a great feeling when coming home from a networking event and looking at the stack of business cards you have collected. You even spoke at length to many of the card-donators. Some, it can be a little difficult to recall who they actually were. "Now was he the tall fellow with the bad hair piece… or was he…?" You've probably experienced that scenario more than once. And you know what… perhaps some of the business people that you gave your precious business card to have been thinking something similar. Hopefully not about your bad hair though.

For effective business networking I recommend the quality over quantity method of networking. Some would say that networking is a numbers game, the more that you meet the higher the chances of your meeting someone that can benefit you. Take for example that you are meeting someone for the first time and if the setting and conditions permit, they deliver their elevator pitch and you return with yours. Then comes the awkward moment, what to say next. You can either carry on conversing about something of no consequence "Nice day, eh?" until one of you tires of it or you can explore common interests. Assuming that you have a common interest I would suggest that you take the lead in the conversation in getting the other to expand upon the commonality or something that they had previously said.

Many networkers make the mistake of trying to sell their product or themselves at this juncture. Your goal should be to arrange to meet them at another time, perhaps for coffee, to discuss those common areas further. Even though many of us are electronically connected to our offices by our smart phones and can likely check to see if we are available at a certain date and time to make a coffee date, we likely won't. When you suggest meeting for coffee, later, if the person is willing to set up a date and time, on the spot, I would go with it. Location can always be determined later by e-mail.

If they aren't willing to set a time and date, I would refer to their business card and say something to the effect of "Can I reach you at this e-mail? I'll contact you next week and see if we can set up a time to get together for a quick coffee." Unfortunately, for many networkers, this is as far as they go. They don't do the follow-up. Life gets busy, there is always one more thing to do with your business and before you know it you have lost the window of opportunity. There is a strong possibility that the individual that you were networking with also has a list of people they are following up with and other commitments. It is far too easy to get left by the wayside if you don't take action to stand out from the others.

At a recent morning meeting of a Business Referral Group that I belonged to we discussed the issue of follow up. A fellow member related that in his experience, if you actually follow-up with a lead, it puts you way ahead of those that don't. He makes a practice of following up with a networking connection within three days of the original meeting and says that it is amazing how many people have said "You know, you are one of the few that actually follows up." Yes, following up can help you stand out from the competition.

The coffee get together is the opportunity for each of you to share your business details and determine if there is enough reason to continue at another time to develop your relationship further and ideally to do business together.

You might ask "I've contacted them three times by e-mail and even left a couple voice mails but they haven't gotten back to me. What do I do next?" There could be a legitimate reason for them not getting back to you. Life happens! But they could be acting non-assertively and are actively avoiding you. I would have to respond with "If that was true, is that someone that you really want to network with or to do business with?" If you are to continue it could easily label you as a stalker.

One suggestion may be to add them to your tickler file. A couple weeks down the road, ignoring the fact that they haven't acknowledged you yet, you would be justified in sending them a message something like "I just noticed that we didn't get together a few weeks ago like we said we would. Where did the time go? It seems to be picking up speed. Last time we met we were discussing our common interests of... Are you still interested in getting together?" If you still don't receive a response, I would put them in the "inactive" file.

When it comes to networking, to stand out from your competition, remember to follow-up.

～

70. I WOULD LIKE TO INTRODUCE
...

A common anxiety-producing situation in a shy networker is when a third or more persons join the conversation and it falls upon them to introduce everyone.

Who do you introduce first? Do you use first and last names? Are you required to provide collateral information about each of the people that you introduce?

Life is getting a lot more casual these days, at least in North America but I am sure that my etiquette expert friends would agree that there is basic protocol that should be followed when making introductions.

Shaking hands upon meeting: Shaking hands upon meeting someone for the first time has become commonplace and is to be expected. Even if the other person is well known to you it is quite acceptable to shake hands in greeting if you haven't seen them for a while. Gender and age used to determine who reached out first but that has gone by the wayside. If you are sitting when introduced to someone for the first time it is appropriate to stand first unless you are in a restaurant or another setting that would make it difficult to do so.

Introducing peers to each other: As they are on the same social level it really doesn't matter who you introduce first. Use both their first and last names when introducing them unless you don't know the last name. "John Smith this is Jane Walker. Jane works in our marketing division. And if I'm not mistaken John you used to work in marketing didn't you?" Pronounce the names clearly so that it is easily understood and if you can provide a little collateral information about each of them do so. If you are aware of some common areas that the two individuals share it can be a great way to seed a conversation i.e. get it going.

Introducing a Superior to a Subordinate: I have some personal difficulties with the term *superior* if it means that they are better than me, my personal baggage. On the other hand, if it refers to the fact that they are higher up on the organizational chart than I am or perhaps more prominent in government, I can accept that. Rule of thumb is that you say the name of the superior first. "Mr. Smith I would like you to meet James Jones. He works in our Refreshments Division." The same idea applies where you would supply some additional information to seed a future conversation or to help create a point of reference to the one that is receiving the introduction.

Introducing a customer to people in your business: The old adage of "the customer always comes first" holds true in this situation. It is a good way to respect your customer. As in other introductions it is helpful to provide some collateral information about the customer or even your business member that you are introducing. It can also be a good time to do a quick testimonial about some aspect of your business dealings with your customer.

Introducing Women: The old way of doing so was to introduce a man to a woman. "Mary I would like you to meet John." You won't create an international incident if you were to do so but nowadays the trend seems to be to use rank as your rule. If you don't know who holds the so-called superiority, I would revert back to the old rule of man to woman. If anybody questions you, you could always say that you didn't get the memo about the changes.

Introducing Older People: The old rule was to introduce the younger person to the older one, saying the name of the older person first. Now it is not so important.

~

A WISE MAN WILL MAKE MORE OPPORTUNITIES THAN HE FINDS. — SIR Francis Bacon (1561- 1626)

OPPORTUNITIES MULTIPLY AS THEY ARE SEIZED. — SUN TZU

OBSTACLES ARE THOSE FRIGHTFUL THINGS YOU SEE WHEN YOU TAKE your eyes off the goal. — Henry Ford (1863-1947)

WHETHER YOU THINK THAT YOU CAN OR THAT YOU CAN'T YOU ARE usually right. — Henry Ford (1863-1947)

NOTHING IS PARTICULARLY HARD IF YOU DIVIDE IT INTO SMALL JOBS. — Henry Ford (1863-1947)

WE ARE ALL IN THE GUTTER BUT SOME OF US ARE LOOKING AT THE stars. — Oscar Wilde (1854-1900)

71. FINDING COMMON INTERESTS: POWER NETWORKING TIPS & TECHNIQUES

Meeting somebody for the first time as in a networking situation can often leave you stuck for words. Your counterpart delivers their elevator pitch and then as they pause to catch their breath they utter "so what do you do?" You go on to deliver your well rehearsed pitch for your business. But did the two of you really communicate?

Communication is a two way process. While the other person is sharing their story, you need to be listening closely to them. This isn't the time to be practicing your own story in your head. This is the time to listen. Imagine that there will be a test after your partner delivers their personal story. Besides trying to figure out what their business is about, you should be listening for statements or beliefs that are similar to yours. Perhaps you have had similar experiences as they have described.

Research has shown that people like to do business with people that are similar to themselves. It is also often said that people will do business with friends before strangers. So how do you rapidly turn an impromptu exchange of elevator pitches into a "best buddies" scenario?

Well, sometimes it does happen by accident. You will meet somebody and very rapidly find that you hit it off as the saying goes. If you are a law of attraction follower, you would say that you are resonating. You are on the same wave length. But more often than naught it doesn't go that way and can be awkward at best.

The solution lays in you taking charge of the conversation. By charge, I don't mean to take control and dominate it at the others expense. I mean to be proactive and direct the conversation in the way that you want it to go. Research has also shown that people respond well when you ask them questions about something that they have just said, asking them to expand upon a point perhaps. The usual questions of who, how, why, when and where can be used to elicit further info effectively as long as you don't come across as giving them the third degree. "Where were you on the night of ...? Can anybody vouch for your whereabouts" may not be the way to win friends and influence people.

Asking more questions of the person is also a highly recommended traditional sales communication method i.e. that you use the information that you have just gathered to tailor your sales pitch for the individual. While that may be okay if you are actually in a sales situation I wouldn't recommend it in first-contact networking encounter. As I said *most* people will respond well to probing questions as long as they feel that you are eager to learn more from them. You will know fairly quickly if you are dealing with a paranoid individual. They are out there.

Once you determine whether you have common interests, don't forget to talk about the possibility of doing business together or helping each other with referrals.

Who knows, you may start off business networking and end up with a new best friend.

∽

72. NAME DROPPING FOR FUN & PROFIT: POWER NETWORKING TIPS & TECHNIQUES

Does this sound familiar? You are at a business networking session and you are captivated by a speaker who wants to regale you with a litany of important people that they have supposedly recently spent time with. "Oh, the other day I had coffee with the Mayor..." "I was just saying the very same thing to my good friend XXX, you know that he owns half the town." "Yeah, my best friend is the Crown Attorney and she was telling me..."

To coin a phrase... "blah, blah, blah, yaddey, yaddey, yaddey!"

I suppose that it is a fact of life that we need to accept. There are some people in life that need to name drop to build up their ego or their sense of importance. On the other hand, I have met some people that are so narcissistic that it would never occur to them that their listener doesn't know the individuals that have been offered as proof of something, nor would even care if they did know them.

Having worked in mental health/psychiatry for 35+ years I have learned at least one concept that has served me well and that is "all behaviour has meaning." The challenge is that we don't often know what the meaning is or what purpose it is serving and likely the other individual doesn't either.

A person who has a tendency to drop names of important people into conversation, and the term "important" is subjective, could be nervous or lack self-confidence in a 1-1 conversation. Talking about "important" people could be a maladaptive coping mechanism, one to relieve the individual's anxiety. If the person they are talking about is well known or popular the concept seems to be that some of that popularity will rub off on them. It is probably similar to bragging about one's self.

Once you recognize that the individual is monopolizing the conversation and playing a game of "look who I know!" what do you do about it?

Not taking action is one choice. You could continue to listen to the one-sided conversation. Odds are if they have dropped some names into conversation they likely have quite a few more to offer. It would probably be a good idea to extricate yourself by excusing yourself before you doze off.

Another option could be to derail the conversation i.e. take it off its likely track by saying something to the effect of "Oh you know XXX. I have been wanting to meet them for a while. Could you introduce us or arrange a meeting?" This action on your part could have a positive outcome if the individual actually does know the V.I.P. and can introduce you to them. Or if they don't really know them, they may start to back paddle i.e. change the topic or avoid the request made of them and keep the conversation going in a direction where they continue to own it.

A third option could be a variation of the old "See you later alligator!" At a business networking function odds are high that you can leave this one-sided conversation and move on to a more productive one.

Is there a time when it is appropriate for *you* to name drop? Yes, I believe so. Name dropping or inserting another person's name into the conversation can help build your credibility as someone who is well-connected, one who has a good understanding on a particular topic and it can even develop your personal influence.

Some examples might be:

- When having a conversation about a particular topic, issue or problem and you know someone who has faced a similar situation, you could mention their name and describe the lessons that they learned as they dealt with the subject.
- You could offer your services as an intermediary and propose to introduce the person that you are speaking with to someone that you know that could be in a position to assist them.
- At a later date, perhaps at a "getting to know you" coffee meeting you could explore with each other who each of you knows and if there is a possibility that any of these connections could be of value in helping with a current need.

I hope that through this article I have been able to raise your awareness to the "name-dropper" style of networker and offer you some ideas on how to deal with them. But then again … name dropping can be an effective networking tool if used effectively. Try it out and see how it works for you. Even better still … become one of those people that other people fit into their conversations.

∾

73. CLOSE ENCOUNTERS OF THE NETWORKING KIND: POWER NETWORKING TIPS & TECHNIQUES

Have you ever wondered how close to stand to another person when conversing in a 1 to 1 at a business networking session? Okay, maybe I do have too much spare time as they say but I am sure that this is a question that many people have asked.

While I don't have a definitive answer, I do have some thoughts on the matter. Many factors including gender, culture, trust, past experiences and self-confidence come into play.

Looking at it from a self-defence, self-preservation perspective, it is helpful to think of each of us having an invisible circle or a safety zone around us. As a preservation measure we tend to keep strangers outside of our safety zone and only let people we trust or are comfortable with into our comfort zone.

In North America our personal safety zone tends to be about three feet in diameter around us. The same distance as our outstretched arm and fist or our outstretched leg if we were intending to strike or kick someone in self-defence. Our comfort zone i.e. the area where we will let those that we trust into tends to be about 18 to 30 inches in diameter.

In a business networking session I'm sure that we don't attend with the idea that we are going to have to physically defend ourselves. I believe that this is a situation that can cause stress in some people in networking situations. To have an effective discussion with someone who you are meeting for the first time as in a business networking session often means that you are permitting a stranger to enter your comfort zone. Crowded, noisy rooms tend to necessitate drawing in closer to the other person just to be able to hear them well.

While it is socially acceptable for women to hold or touch each other while in conversation, even in a first meeting encounter, the same cannot be said about two men conversing.

You may not even be aware that you have a comfort zone until someone invades it. That feeling of anxiousness, uneasiness may be your subconscious calling to your attention that something isn't right. Perhaps that is the time to take a step backwards to continue your conversation.

If you are confident in your networking conversations, allowing others into your comfort zone and paying close attention to the conversation by actively participating in it can go a long way in building your reputation as an effective networker and somebody worth meeting and getting to know.

Many networkers have challenges of inserting themselves into groups that have already formed and are actively discussing a topic. A group that the members are standing close enough to converse with each other, yet not within each other's comfort zones, would likely be a group that would be open to having someone else join them. On the other hand, two people standing very close together, perhaps a little ways away from the rest of the group would seem to be having an intimate conversation and would not likely be open to someone joining them. If they were to separate from each other that could indicate that the private or intimate stage of their conversation has concluded and they were now open to be joined by others.

You can learn a lot be observing others. In your next networking session observe how people are standing. Are they close together or far apart? Does an individual networker use the same technique with everyone they meet or do they vary their closeness in conversation. Try out some different distances to your conversational partner and see how it feels to you.

∿

ABOUT THE AUTHOR

Rae A. Stonehouse is a Canadian born author & speaker.

His professional career as a Registered Nurse working predominantly in psychiatry/mental health, has spanned four decades.

Rae has embraced the principal of CANI (Constant and Never-ending Improvement) as promoted by thought leaders such as Tony Robbins and brings that philosophy to each of his publications and presentations.

Rae has dedicated the latter segment of his journey through life to overcoming his personal inhibitions. As a 25+ year member of Toast-masters International he has systematically built his self-confidence and communicating ability. He is passionate about sharing his lessons with his readers and listeners.

His publications thus far are of the self-help, self-improvement genre and systematically offer valuable sage advice on a specific topic.

His writing style can be described as being conversational. As an author, Rae strives to have a one-to-one conversation with each of his readers, very much like having your own personal self-development coach.

Rae is known for having a wry sense of humour that features in his publications. To learn more about Rae A. Stonehouse, visit the Wonderful World of Rae Stonehouse at http://raestonehouse.com.

～

facebook.com/rae.stonehouse

twitter.com/raestonehouse

ALSO BY RAE A. STONEHOUSE

Power Networking for Shy People: Tips & Techniques for Moving from Shy to Sly! http://powernetworkingforshypeople.com

∼

PROtect Yourself! Empowering Tips & Techniques for Personal Safety: A Practical Violence Prevention Manual for Healthcare Workers http://protectyourselfnow.ca/

∼

E=Emcee Squared: Tips & Techniques to Becoming a Dynamic Master of Ceremonies http://emceesquared.mremcee.com/

∼

Power of Promotion: On-line Marketing for Toastmasters Club Growth

http://powerofpromotion.ca/

∼

You're Hired! Job Search Strategies That Work (This is the complete program)

E-book & Paperback: Available @ https://books2read.com/yourehired

On-line E-course: (Available as a self-directed or instructor-led program)

~

You're Hired! Resume Tactics: Job Search Strategies That Work

E-book & Paperback: Available @ : https://books2read.com/resumetactics

On-line E-course: http://liveforexcellenceacademy.com/

~

Job Interview Preparation: Job Search Strategies That Work

E-book & Paperback: Available @ books2read.com/jobinterviewpreparation

On-line E-course: http://liveforexcellenceacademy.com/

~

You're Hired! Leveraging Your Network: Job Search Strategies That Work

E-book & Paperback: Available @ http://books2read.com/leveragingyournetwork

On-line E-course: http://liveforexcellenceacademy.com/

~

You're Hired! Power Tactics: Job Search Strategies That Work (This is a box set containing the complete content of Resume Tactics, Job Interview Preparation & Leveraging Your Network)

E-book Available @ http://books2read.com/powertactics

~

If you have found this book and program to be helpful, please leave us a warm review wherever you purchased this book.

www.ingramcontent.com/pod-product-compliance
Lightning Source LLC
Chambersburg PA
CBHW071159210326
41597CB00016B/1607